GETTING STARTED

Money Matters for Under-25s

GETTING STARTED

Money Matters for Under-25s

Bruce Cameron

ZEBRA

Published by Zebra Press
an imprint of Struik Publishers
(a division of New Holland Publishing (South Africa) (Pty) Ltd)
PO Box 1144, Cape Town, 8000
New Holland Publishing is a member of Johnnic Publishing Ltd

First published 2003

1 3 5 7 9 10 8 6 4 2

Publication © Zebra Press 2003
Text © Bruce Cameron 2003

Cover photographs © Paul Viant/Photo Access

PUBLISHING MANAGER: Marlene Fryer
MANAGING EDITOR: Robert Plummer
EDITOR: Ronel Richter-Herbert
TEXT AND COVER DESIGNER: Natascha Adendorff
TYPESETTER: Natascha Adendorff

Set in 10.5 pt on 14.5 pt ITC Officina Sans

Reproduction by Hirt & Carter (Cape) (Pty) Ltd
Printed and bound by CTP Book Printers

ISBN 1 86872 666 5

www.zebrapress.co.za

Log on to our photographic website www.imagesofafrica.co.za for an African experience

DISCLAIMER
The information in this book (current July 2002) is given in good faith and has been derived from
sources believed to be accurate. Among other things, laws affecting all aspects of personal financial
planning are subject to constant change. Although the utmost care has been taken by the author
and the publisher, no warranty of reliability or accuracy can be given. Neither the authors, the
publisher nor the distributor can be held responsible for any errors or omissions; or for any liability
for any action taken or not taken by any individual or organisation. The material contained in this
book is not intended for professional individual financial advice and it is recommended that you
consult a professional financial adviser before making any investment or other decisions that could
affect your financial well-being.

Contents

Foreword

by the Minister of Education

One is never too young to learn the basics about money, from its seductive allure to its dormant dangers. Money is far more than merely a means to an end. It empowers, enriches and transforms, but it can just as easily mislead, impoverish and destroy.

In his ground-breaking book *Getting Started: Money Matters for Under-25s*, Bruce Cameron expertly and adroitly guides the young reader through the financial quicksand that can so greedily and easily claim its victims. Whilst cautioning against monetary minefields such as the dreaded debt trap, the book boldly encourages adventurism and even risk taking, but not without clearly pointing out the various risks and possible pitfalls attached to each type of investment loan.

Cameron, the 2001 winner of the Personal Finance category in the Sanlam Awards for Excellence in Financial Journalism, has followed up his last book, *Financial Freedom for Women*, with another very good read. This is a book that teaches principles and ideals that will apply not only in the teen years, but throughout adulthood. The author has succeeded admirably in this aim, and is spot on with his assertion that mistakes made in later life so often arise from not having learnt the basics of financial planning and saving whilst in your teens and early twenties.

In the National Curriculum Statement, which will come into force in 2004, Business Management is a new learning field. Cameron's book, lucidly written, will be very useful.

Containing tips about everything from saving for that first bicycle to the judicious use of a credit card, and blunt warnings about scams such as the infamous pyramid schemes, this excellent and thought-provoking publication is a must read for young people. Particularly pleasing is the fact that Cameron stresses the importance of saving and budgeting for education, stating that 'Education is the single major issue in your future financial success.'

In later chapters the book comprehensively covers aspects such as finding a job, how to start your own business, your rights and responsibilities as an employee, your first home away from home, saving for and ultimately owning your first motor car, and, of course, the vital financial issues of medical aid, insurance and tax.

If you can't afford this book yet, my advice is to start saving for it right now.

Professor Kader Asmal, MP

Acknowledgements

This is a book that I have essentially written for myself. It is the type of book I would have liked to have had before I left school. But it is also a book that is based on my experiences of being involved in the development of my three children: Brett, now an actuary; Kate, a science graduate; and her twin sister, Nikki, an information systems graduate. I am immensely proud of all three.

This book answers many of the questions they have asked over the years, and it also contains information they have given me.

As editor of the Independent Newspapers publication *Personal Finance*, I have become very aware that many of the mistakes made by individuals in their financial planning are as a result of not knowing any better. The place where they should have learnt what was best was, in fact, in school.

In many ways the problems of readers of *Personal Finance* have also contributed to the book, and so I acknowledge their assistance. There are also very many people in the financial industry with whom I have interchanges on a daily basis. The number of experts whose opinions I value highly and with whom I have dealt over the years are too numerous to list, but they know who they are and I thank them all for their patience.

There are also the financial services companies who have over the years provided research used in this book. Predominant have been Discovery, Investec, Liberty Life, Old Mutual and Sanlam. My thanks to Sanlam as well for sponsoring this book. I would particularly like to mention Jimmy Makgato and Esann de Kock at Sanlam.

I also wish to thank the people who have been more directly involved with the book, namely my wife Lynne, who helped check the draft script and asked questions that needed to be answered; my stepdaughter Ali, together with Nikki and Kate, for helping with the chapter on working overseas; and the publishers, Zebra Press, an imprint of Struik. In particular at Zebra I would like to mention my editor, Ronel Richter-Herbert, who re-taught me some basic lessons in grammar and did an excellent editing job, as well as Marlene Fryer, Georgina Hatch, Robert Plummer and Natascha Adendorff.

Introduction

Warren Buffett, known as the sage of Omaha, and one of the richest people alive today, started off his money-making career selling newspapers. Today, Buffett is worth more than R200 billion. That is about half the money our government spent in 2002 to keep the whole of South Africa running.

Warren Buffett did not get rich because he was lucky. He got rich because he followed some basic rules. He realised that:

- Education was one of the best things he could own;
- You need to work hard;
- It is better to work for yourself, employing other people, than to work for someone else;
- Earning a lot of money does not mean much if you are spending it all; and
- If you save money, the money you save starts working for you, making you even more money.

This book is not about how you too can become a Warren Buffett. The amount of money that he has managed to put together is as unusual as it is amazing. This book is aimed at giving you the knowledge to ensure that you can achieve many of the things that you can only dream about now.

One thing you need to accept right now is that there is no magic system. Reaching your goals will entail hard work and proper planning.

This book is about **Money**: how to earn it; how to save it; how to spend it; how to grow it; how to borrow it; and even how to give it away. This book is not about how to become a millionaire in 10 easy steps. If anyone had that type of formula, they would never share it with us. To be financially independent means hard work and self-discipline. But it also means having fun along the way. This book will help you to structure your finances without having to live like a hermit in sackcloth. The better structured your personal finances are, the more fun and less worries you will have.

While this book has been written for you at the age you are now, the principles and ideas you will learn will remain the same for the rest of your life. They are as right for you now as they are for your parents.

It is essential that you are better prepared than most parents. Many people who have retired during the past 20 years and many people who will retire soon simply do not have enough money to keep them financially secure throughout their retirement years.

The people who are retiring financially secure are those who made plans early, understood the importance of money and how to manage it. You may wonder why retirement is even mentioned in a book for someone under the age of 25. Well, it's important. If you speak to someone who is struggling financially in retirement, you will probably find it is because of the mistakes they made in their financial planning while in their twenties and thirties.

Statistics are bandied about that only one in 10 matriculants in South Africa will get a job in the formal employment sector.

But getting a job with only a matric certificate is an increasingly difficult thing to achieve. This is not only the case in South Africa, but also in most other parts of the world. Technology and knowledge accelerate at such a pace that in most cases you not only need further education after leaving school (particularly of a more specialised nature), but also on an ongoing basis throughout your life. Most people will have to create their own jobs.

To get it right:

• Start mapping out your financial future today.
• Start learning about how to control your own finances.

- Have financial goals.
- Have a financial plan, which you must update on a regular basis.
- Keep a budget.
- Keep debt to an absolute minimum.
- Save at least 10 percent, but preferably more, of everything you earn.
- Always spend less than you earn.
- Invest in your education.
- Always research and understand any financial recommendation made to you.
- Protect yourself by being properly insured.
- Do not gamble.
- Choose advisers carefully.
- Make your own financial decisions.
- Do all you can not to be dependent on anyone else to survive.
- Take ownership of your own life.

Having a Plan

Understanding Money

Money is simply a convenient way of exchanging goods and services. It really has no value in itself. It's the things that you can buy or sell that have the value. Look at it this way: if you were given R200 about 25 years ago you could have paid for an overseas air ticket. Now you are lucky to be able to get a tank full of petrol. So, it is not money that has value, but the goods or services you buy.

However, because money is used to make the exchange of items of value easier, you do need money. But money no longer only means those notes and coins in your wallet or purse.

Money is fast becoming different from the first coin money made in the Kingdom of Lydia (now Turkey) more than 2 600 years ago, or the cowrie shells that were used in the Pacific Islands. More and more, money is only an esoteric concept, an intangible, because we seldom pay cash for things we buy. We use things such as cheques, credit cards and electronic transfers. Few people are even paid in cash nowadays. Your bank account is merely credited.

One day in the not too distant future the only money you will see will be in museums.

There are only four legal ways to get money. One is to be given it, another to borrow it, yet another to earn it and the fourth is to get your savings to work for you. Some of us will be lucky in that we may be given money (for instance, you could inherit money when your parents or grandparents die), but for most of us the money we will receive in our lifetime will come from working for it.

AN ALLOWANCE (POCKET MONEY)

For most of us, our first source of income is pocket money or an allowance. Some teenagers have to work for their pocket money by doing chores around the house, while others seem to be given enough to go on regular spending sprees at the local mall.

One thing you should get used to now is that your parents are not a reliable source of money into the future. They have to look after themselves first. They have to make choices on how they want to spend their money, and your pocket money is only one of numerous demands. They may consider that paying for your education is and was their top priority, and that may leave little for luxuries such as pocket money.

One way to negotiate a better allowance is to offer to take on extra chores in return for more money. But don't become totally mercenary, wanting money before you are prepared to do anything around the house. Remember that your parents can also stop doing things for you. Set time aside with your parents to discuss your allowance, and what and how you can go about getting a deal that is fair to both you and them.

Next time you negotiate your allowance, why not suggest that you will save a percentage of it – say, 15 percent? Then for every two rands you save your parents will put another rand into savings for you. If you withdraw the money before a set time (say, when you are 21) or reaching a goal (such as buying a motor car), you will have to pay back your parents R1.25 for every rand you withdraw. So, there is an incentive to save and a penalty for withdrawing.

Increasingly, teenagers and students are having to take part-time jobs to supplement allowances and to pay for any luxuries, and often even essentials, such as assisting in paying for a tertiary (post-school) education. For many people, having an evening and/or weekend job is the only way of getting an education without becoming heavily indebted. Even more enterprising people have started businesses as students. This is how Bill Gates started off. He laid the foundations of what has now become the multi-billion dollar technology company, Microsoft, while at university.

The important issue is that you need to know what you need and want, and how you are going to get there.

HAVING A PLAN

In order to have sufficient money on which to live and to meet your goals, you will need a plan. Money in your pocket or even in the bank does not necessarily mean that you are wealthy. It may be sufficient to buy what you need today, but it will not be enough for what you need and want even 12 months from now, let alone in five years' time. And if you owe more money than you have in the bank or in your pocket, it is not even yours, but belongs to someone else.

If you want to have money for things that you cannot afford now but intend to own in the future, you need a plan. When you are in your teens and do not have much money you need a savings plan, but as your needs and wants get bigger, and as you start earning an income and must support yourself, your needs and wants become more complex. The result is that you need a more structured and complex financial plan.

Unless you have a financial plan you will never know where you are going, how you are going to get there and even when you will arrive. Having a financial plan is not merely a case of saying, 'I want to be a nuclear scientist earning R100 000 a month.' It is a bit more complex than that.

If you are 15, living with your parents and receiving pocket money, and you want a motorbike when you are 18, you will need a simple financial plan with which you can work out how much you need to save and how soon you will reach your target. When you are older and need to support yourself, your financial planning will become more complex. You are not only faced with planning for an increasing number of goals, such as a new car, an apartment, furniture and/or a trip overseas, but you must also ensure that you have enough money for day-to-day living.

Planning does not mean that you must make up your mind now about your whole life. Deciding how you will structure your life financially when you are 15 or even 25, and then sticking rigidly to that plan until the day you die, is highly unlikely to happen. South African-born international hotelier and casino operator Sol Kerzner is hardly likely to have imagined the extent of his interests when he entered his first year of studies as a chartered accountant. The important issue is to have a plan that will give you general goals and be able to adapt it as you go through life.

Very few people, in fact, finally do the jobs they planned at age 15, and a fair number change course, often quite dramatically, at some stage of their lives. Take Cyril Ramaphosa, who started off as a lawyer in the trade union movement, became part of the negotiating team of the African National Congress that led to the election of the first democratic government in South Africa, and is now a leading businessman, heading one of South Africa's major companies.

Many plans are upset or altered because of the opportunities that arise. Most opportunities you create for yourself. The trick is to recognise the opportunities and to be able to amend your plans in order to grab them with both hands. But you also need to be sure that you are not endlessly chasing a pot of gold at the end of a rainbow. Your plans and goals must be realistic, so that you do not risk all you have built up just to lose it with a silly decision.

So, where do you start with planning your life? You start by getting to know yourself.

Most people don't plan to fail — they fail to plan

Financial failure is not only caused by stupidity. Look at nearly every financial failure, and almost without doubt you will find the cause is a lack of realistic and proper planning. This applies as much to an individual as it does to a business venture. If you have a well-constructed plan you are more likely to succeed.

People who do not have proper plans face the following problems:

- They do not know where they are financially;
- They do not know how to budget;
- They do not have short-term and long-term financial goals;
- They do not have consistent savings plans;
- They do not know about investments;
- They lack the confidence or self-discipline to make decisions;
- They are afraid of making mistakes and depend on others;
- They are never sure who to trust because they have done no homework for themselves;

- They do not know how to get help;
- They are not realistic. They dream about what life will be like but do little to make the dream come true; and
- They procrastinate, leaving everything until tomorrow. *!!! DO IT NOW!*

Someone once said that the world is populated by two types of people: those who plan and make things happen, and those without a plan, who wonder what happened as the world goes whizzing past.

To develop a financial plan you must know where you are financially at any given moment in order to ensure that your plan to be wealthy will work. There are six key issues that you need to know about your finances. These are:

- How much money you receive from any source; *— JOBS INCOME*
- How much you pay out; *— SALARIES EXPENSES*
- How much you are owed; *— PEOPLE WHO BORROWED FROM U*
- How much you owe; *DEBDT YOU MAKE*
- How much you own; and *ASSEST*
- Your financial goals. *WHAT U WANT DO BE HAVE.*

THE FOUR STEPS TO MEETING YOUR FINANCIAL GOALS

In working out a financial plan you must follow four steps:

1. SET YOUR GOALS

Your goals are your ultimate destination. You need to set goals in order to have a route map to get there. The planning process (your route map) will help you to establish whether your goals are realistic, and whether and when you need to change them.

You should divide your goals into various categories. There are short-term goals, medium-term goals and long-term goals. These goals will obviously change as you get older.

Short-term goals: Most short-term goals are mainly for things that you need rather than what you want. They include such things as paying for education, having an emergency fund (this is particularly important if you are supporting yourself) and buying a motor vehicle for transport.

Medium-term goals: These goals can consist of both needs and wants. They include such things as saving to buy a property or starting a business.

Long-term goals: These goals mainly occur when you have started working, and include such things as the education of children and saving for retirement.

You should list your goals with an estimate of how much you expect each to cost.

2. YOUR BUDGET

A budget is not only a plan on how you *will* spend your money, but is also a record of how you *have* spent your money. To prepare a budget is fairly simple, particularly if you can use a computer spreadsheet. A budget is a list of your income (what you receive from any source) and what you spend.

The advantages of budgeting correctly include:

- An awareness of where your money is going;
- Indicators of where you went wrong in the past;
- Forcing you to make considered choices (for example, the decision to buy something should not be made on the shop floor but within a properly considered plan);
- Helping you to plan for the future; and
- Helping you to know whether your plans are realistic.

There are four fundamental rules to correct budgeting. These are:

- **Keep your budget realistic:** Budgeting will not help you to control your finances if you do not keep it realistic. If there are to be any exaggerations, then underestimate your income and overestimate your spending. If you do the opposite you will get yourself into trouble. To help you keep your budget realistic you should always have two columns of figures. The first column is what you have budgeted. The second column is what actually happened. This will help you to make adjustments to your budget and establish where you are going wrong. It becomes much easier to identify where you may be overspending and putting your finances out of kilter.
- **Income must always exceed spending:** If you are budgeting correctly, your income will always exceed your spending. If not, you are digging yourself into a debt trap that will strangle any chance you have of becoming wealthy. Always work on having a surplus of income over

spending. Do not budget to spend every cent you receive. Leave a margin of about 5 percent if you possibly can.

- **Get your priorities right:** The best place to start is to understand the difference between a need and a want. A need is transport to get to university or work; a want is to get there in a top-of-the-range sports car.
- **Pay yourself first:** You must see savings as part of spending, but the good thing about savings is that it is spending on yourself.

AN EXAMPLE OF A BUDGET

My Budget

Date:

INCOME:	BUDGETED	ACTUAL
Source:	R	R
Source:	R	R
Total Income:	**R**	**R**

(Note: Income must be net – the actual amount you receive after tax and other deductions.)

EXPENDITURE (SPENDING)	BUDGETED	ACTUAL
Repayment of debt:		
University/technikon loan:	R	R
Other:	R	R
Savings:		
Savings for short-term goals:	R	R
(e.g. a hi-fi set)		
Savings for medium-term goals:	R	R
(e.g. a motor vehicle)		
Savings for long-term goals		
(e.g. property)		
Needs: (These are items on which you must spend money)		
Transport costs:	R	R
Food:	R	R
Rent:	R	R
Electricity and water:	R	R
Essential clothing:	R	R
Toiletries:	R	R
Other:	R	R
Wants: (These are items that are not necessities)		
Entertainment:	R	R
Fashion clothing:	R	R
Other:	R	R
Total Spending:	**R**	**R**
What is left over:	R	R

3. YOUR BALANCE SHEET

A balance sheet tells you how wealthy you are. It is simply a list of your assets (everything you own and are owed) and your liabilities (everything you owe).

You must strive at all times to have a minimum of liabilities and a maximum of assets. Having a balance sheet will help you to avoid another fundamental mistake made by many people, namely confusing high income with wealth. People earning high salaries can be extremely poor because they have high debt, while someone earning a low income can be quite

---

MY BALANCE SHEET

My Assets (what I own)

ASSET	VALUE
Short-Term Assets	
Money owed to me	
Owed by:..	R
Bank savings accounts	
Account No.:............................. Bank............................	R
Account No.:............................. Bank............................	R
Motor vehicle (trade-in value)..	R
Other short-term assets: (only reflect saleable value)	
Asset	R
Total Short-Term Assets:	**R**
Long-Term Assets	
Unit trust funds:	
Unit trust account No.: .... Fund............................	R
Life assurance policies (Investments only):	
Policy No.: .... Company........................	R
Shares	
Company:	R
Property:	R
Any other savings/investments:..	R
Total Long-Term Assets:	**R**
Total Assets	**R**

wealthy because they have built up their assets. The true measure of wealth is the extent to which the value of your assets is greater than your debts.

Your balance sheet will provide you with warning signs about your financial health. Danger signs to watch out for:

- If your liabilities (debts) exceed your assets, or your liabilities are equal to more than three-quarters of your assets, you are in desperate trouble. The amount you pay in interest every month will be making it impossible to get ahead. This situation is known as a debt trap. You will have to reduce your standard of living substantially and consider selling assets to reduce your debt load.

My Liabilities (what I owe)

LIABILITY	VALUE
Short-Term Liabilities	
Student loan:..	R
Credit card:	R
Store cards	
Company:..	R
Hire purchase	
Contract:...	R
Motor vehicle loan:..	R
Accounts	
Electricity and water accounts:...................................	R
Other short-term liabilities:	
Debt to	R
Total Short-Term Liabilities	**R**
Long-Term Liabilities	
Property:	
Home loan:..	R
Other long-term liabilities:	
Debt to	R
Total Short-Term Liabilities	**R**
Total Liabilities	**R**
My Net Worth	
Total Assets:	R
less: Total Liabilities:	R
= **Net Worth:**	**R**

- If you are building up debt to pay for your current living expenses, such as rent, food or clothing, you are getting yourself into trouble.

You should work towards having no liabilities. You should always attempt to keep your liabilities below half the value of your assets. When you are younger this is obviously more difficult, as you have not had time to build up your assets.

4. PULLING IT ALL TOGETHER

Now that you know how much you have and how much you want and need, you have to pull it all together. The key to the success of any financial plan is to know what you need and how much you can afford. The affordability of any plan is essential. You also need to list what goals have priority. If proper priority is not given to your different needs and wants in terms of affordability, your whole plan could well crash. You need to balance your needs with your income and assets.

In other words, say you can afford to save R300 a month, but want to save for both a motorbike, which you need to get to varsity, and an overseas trip. You will have to put saving for the trip on hold for a while.

When your commitments increase, such as getting married and having children, your planning will become more complex and will involve such things as life assurance.

Now that you have your plan and have prioritised your goals, you need to have a properly structured saving and investment strategy, which will be the subject of Chapters 3 and 4.

1. SET YOUR GOALS

2. YOUR BUDGET

3. YOUR BALANCE SHEET

4. PULLING IT ALL TOGETHER

Spending

So you have made some money. Now you face a number of choices. You can spend it, or you can save it, or you can give it away. Surprisingly, just as with everything else to do with your money, you need a spending plan. If you do not have a plan you will find that your money will disappear very quickly, and in all likelihood you will have nothing to show for it.

There are a lot of people out there trying to get you to spend your money so that they can get rich quicker. Pick up a newspaper, switch on the television, visit the mall: everywhere someone is trying to grab your money.

It does not matter how much money you have, you can make your rands go much further if you learn good spending habits from the start. The less money you have, the more important it is that you develop good financial habits.

So, how do you get to control your money? There are five steps to a plan for spending:

1. SET GOALS

There are short-, medium- and long-term goals. For example, buying a new computer could be a short-term goal, saving for a motor car a medium-term goal, and saving to buy a house a long-term goal. You need to decide how much money you are going to set aside every week or every month to meet your goals. These are your savings plans, which will be dealt with in the next chapter. You need to see the amount you set aside for these goals as paying yourself – and that, after paying off debt, is the first thing you should spend your money on when you receive it.

2. NEEDS AND WANTS

All of us would like to have everything, from a Ferrari to the latest fashions. The question is, do we need everything? Very few of us have the mountains of cash that would enable us to buy everything we want, so it is very important to distinguish between needs and wants.

There is **nothing** wrong with satisfying **wants**, but take care of your **needs** first.

An example of a need is a motor vehicle to get to university or tech. A want is a Porsche with which to do it, when a Golf will do the job just as efficiently. Make a list of needs and wants. You don't have to feel guilty about spending money on wants. If we only spent money on needs, life could become very boring. All of us want to have a bit of fun – the only problem is that fun normally costs money. The important thing is to leave spending money on wants until last.

Another way of putting it: compulsory spending (needs) and discretionary spending (wants). Life is all about making choices, and it is no different in our spending. The choice is yours whether you want to eat Big Macs every lunch hour, or rather bring sandwiches from home and save for that motor car.

3. BUDGETING

A budget is the written record of what you are doing with your money. It helps you plan for the future, it helps you keep track of the present, and often it can show you where you went wrong in the past. A budget is not there to stop you getting enjoyment out of life. It is, in fact, there to ensure that you do get enjoyment out of life, and do not lead a life of misery wondering how to get out of debt. Budgets help force you to make choices and to stick to your plans.

When you move out of your parents' home, budgeting becomes even more important, because if you do not plan your spending very carefully you may find yourself out of food by the end of the month. Now you start having to pay for things such as rent, electricity, telephone and water. The basic structure of your budget looks much the same, but it now gets a lot more complex. You need to add in a lot more things, particularly in the expenditure column.

Start off by buying a notebook or setting up a program on your computer. You need to do a budget every month. Don't believe you can keep track of a budget in your head. You cannot.

(See Chapter 1 for how to compile a budget.)

4. AN EMERGENCY FUND

Build up an emergency fund for a crisis. For example, if you have a motor car you may need money in case of an unexpected breakdown, or if you lost your job. It is better to build up an emergency fund than having to borrow money when the unexpected occurs. You should ask yourself: 'What is the worst financial disaster I could face?' The answer will indicate how much you need as an emergency fund.

When you start working, it is a good idea to build up an emergency fund that is equal to at least three months' salary.

5. HOLDING ON TO YOUR MONEY

There is an old saying that a fool and his money are soon parted. People will attempt to fool you into spending your money. It is up to you to know enough so that you do not pay too much or buy inferior goods.

One of the quickest ways to spend your money is impulse buying. Lots of shops bet on you spending your money on impulse. That is why, for example, you will always find sweet racks at the checkout tills at supermarkets.

1. SET GOALS
2. NEEDS AND WANTS
3. BUDGETING
4. AN EMERGENCY FUND
5. HOLDING ON TO YOUR MONEY

LEARN TO BE A SMART CONSUMER

If you plan your purchases, you can find good deals and the best value for money.

Say you are shopping for soapsuds. You will find umpteen brands of soapsuds in your local supermarket. You need to make comparisons.

- Price: This is the first thing to compare. You must not only compare the total price, but also the price per kilogram, which you should find recorded either on the shelf or on the box.
- Weight of the contents: Often you will find a big box with what seems to be a lower price than a smaller box. Compare the weight of the contents.
- Jumbo size: Often with one brand you will be offered a jumbo pack or an economy pack. The implication is that the bigger pack is always cheaper. This is often not the case. Again you must compare the price per kilogram. That will give you the true story.
- Quality: You often pay less but get poorer quality. You need to ask around to establish the better-quality products. This is particularly important when you are buying high-price items, such as a hi-fi set or a computer.
- Different stores: Often you will find that different stores will sell the same item at a different price. The more expensive the item you want, the more you should shop around.
- Advertising: Often you will see advertisements for special offers. Read any such advertisement very carefully and look for any fine print.
- Guarantees (often called a warranty): Different products will have different guarantees. This alone should tell you something about the quality. Say one product has a guarantee of only six months, while another has a guarantee of two years: it tells you how much confidence the producer has in the product. Guarantees come in two forms:
  - A full guarantee, which means no matter what goes wrong your purchase will be repaired, replaced or your money refunded; or
  - A limited guarantee, which means that not everything in the product is guaranteed, or that the guarantee will only be met under certain conditions, or that the parts will be replaced free but you will have to pay for the labour. You should also check on the guarantee policy of the store. Some shops will handle a returned product for you without hassle. Others will expect you to deal with the manufacturer directly.

Always keep your receipts and any guarantee forms. Without them you are unlikely to be able to make a claim if something goes wrong.

Here are 14 other ways to protect your money

Beware of shopping on the street. Street markets are becoming increasingly popular in South Africa. There are some great bargains to be found at street markets, but there are also lots of scams. Among other things, stolen goods and counterfeit big-name designer brands of poor quality are sold. When you buy off the street, in most cases you have very little comeback if things go wrong.

Beware of introductory offers. Introductory offers are often used for things such as music clubs. You pay a very low price for the introductory offer, but the follow-up prices are often as much as or more than you would pay in a normal shop. You are also required to buy a fixed number of articles for at least a year, without being absolutely sure you want what you will be offered.

Pay cash. If you pay cash you can often negotiate a lower price. Never be embarrassed to ask for a cash discount. It is your money you are saving. Point out that if someone bought the product with a credit card, the shop will have to give a discount to the credit card company, so why shouldn't you get a discount as well?

Never send cash through the mail. The money can easily be stolen and you have no proof of payment. If you don't have a cheque account, get a bank cheque or get your parents to give you a cheque. Increasingly you can make payments over the Internet.

Never pay for anything without knowing all the details. Often you will see advertisements asking you to send something like R50 for a magic formula to make you rich. Don't send anything. The only person who will get rich is the person who put the advertisement in the newspaper.

Lift clubs. Try to form lift clubs. If you are forced to use your own transport, find people without transport who will be prepared to pay you weekly to help with your petrol bill.

Books. If you are studying, you will find that books are a major expense. Buy them second-hand, but make sure that you get the right edition. If the rest of the class is studying from edition eight, you don't want to be reading edition two.

Furniture. When setting up your own home for the first time, do not buy furniture on hire purchase. It will cost you a fortune. Rather buy at flea markets, garage sales and at auctions. At auctions, be careful that you do not bid beyond a price that you had already settled on in your mind. Some furnishings you can make yourself, such as using bricks and planks to make bookshelves.

Student discounts. If you are a student, you will find that your student card often entitles you to a student discount. Always ask the store, restaurant, etc. whether they offer student discounts.

Best buys. When shopping for food, be aware that offers at the end of the aisle are not necessarily cheaper. The product producer pays more for the special position. The store brands or no-name brands are often the best buy. Always compare prices.

Coupons. Clip and keep coupons wherever you see them. They can save you quite a bit of money over the long run. Coupons are often also available on supermarket shelves next to the product. But be careful. The price of the product less the discount on the coupon may still be more expensive than a similar product.

Cash. Do not carry large amounts of cash on you. Give yourself a cash budget every week and stick to it. Too much cash in your pocket leads to impulse buying. Most of us find that whatever cash we have in our wallets has an amazing way of disappearing.

Credit cards. Be very wary of credit cards. They can be as easy to use for impulse buying as cash – and you can easily pay for large and expensive items with credit cards. If you have a tendency to spend easily, avoid getting a credit card. More people get into financial trouble by using a credit card indiscriminately than in most other ways. However, if you find it easy to control your spending, a credit card does have its advantages. You can be given up to 50 days' credit and you can also be awarded 'loyalty' points. On most cards nowadays you are credited with air miles with one or other airline. This can be a useful way of getting a cheap holiday.

Store cards. Avoid store cards altogether. They are an even quicker way to buy things on credit that you do not need. Again, it is an easy way to build up debt and get into trouble.

3

Saving and Banking

Saving and investing are similar, but they are not quite the same thing. Saving is about keeping some of the money you earn or receive to build up a lump sum to be used for a particular purpose. Investing is making the money you save work for you to earn more money. But it can also involve putting your savings at risk. Investing and its risks will be dealt with in Chapter 4.

COMPOUND INTEREST

This is the most important item that you will read about in this book. Compound interest is one of the most amazing things in your personal finances. In simple terms, it is a matter of reinvesting whatever interest or growth you get on your savings. You then get further interest on your interest, and so it goes on, building up year after year.

Let me tell you a story about Jack and Jill. Jill started investing R100 a month until she reached the age of 30. At age 30 she stopped saving. At the age of 30 Jack started saving R100 a month. Jack saved R100 a month for the next 30 years, and he never caught up with Jill. The reason was that by the time Jack started saving, the interest Jill was earning on her savings was already more than R100 a month.

The moral of this story is that the sooner you start saving, the sooner you will have that very strong investment friend, Compound Interest, working for you.

Compound interest is the secret of the rich. The reason why the rich get richer is that they do not spend all of their money. The rich invest their money, making them even richer. If you do not start saving and investing from today, you will never be a millionaire. The longer you take to save the first rand, the less likely you are to reach your target. You have age on your side. The younger you are, the better your chances of being really rich. The reason is:

Compound interest is simply another way of saying that you are making your money work for you.

If you save R1 000 and your money earns 10 percent after-tax interest, this is what happens:

End of year 1:	R 1 100	Your money has earned you R100.
End of year 2:	R 1 210	R10 has come from the R100 your money earned last year.
End of year 3:	R 1 331	R21 has come from what your money earned over the previous two years.
End of year 5:	R 1 611	
End of year 8:	R 2 144	You have more than doubled your money.
End of year 10:	R 2 594	
End of year 15:	R 4 177	You have now quadrupled your initial investment.
End of year 20:	R 6 727	You now have more than six times your original capital. This year you have earned R512 in interest alone.
End of year 25:	R10 835	Your original investment of R1 000 is now earning more than R1 000 a year.

You might think that this is a slow accumulation of wealth, but remember that the calculation has been made on saving only a single amount. If you save R1 000 a year the picture alters dramatically:

End of year 1:	R 1 100	An exact copy of what happened above in year one.
End of year 2:	R 2 310	You are already starting to leap ahead.
End of year 3:	R 3 641	You receive R31 from interest on your interest.
End of year 5:	R 6 716	
End of year 7:	R 10 436	By saving R1 000 a year instead of only R1 000 once, you have almost equalled what you took 25 years to achieve. In the process you have actually saved R7 000, but earned R3 436 in interest.
End of year 10:	R 17 531	
End of year 15:	R 34 950	By this year you will have earned almost R20 000 in interest.
End of year 20:	R 63 002	You have earned R3 727 in interest on all the interest you have earned to date.
End of year 25:	R108 182	Now we are talking meaningful money. But remember, you have only saved or invested a mere R25 000. The other R83 182 is all interest your money has made for you. This is what it means when people say that the rich get richer. The rich will always get richer when they let their savings work for them.

Incidentally, to hit a million-rand target based on our calculations so far, you would have to save R10 000 a year for 25 years. That is R833 a month.

THE RULE OF 72

Here is a rough, fun guide to work out the effects of compound interest. It is called the Rule of 72. With this rule you can work out how often your savings or investments can double in value depending on the interest or growth rate.

The Rule of 72 gets its name from the calculation that at a compounded rate of interest of 10 percent your investment doubles every 7.2 years. You can also use the rule to calculate how long it will take your money to double at any given interest rate.

Examples:

At 6 percent, how long will it take to double your money? 72 ÷ 6 = 12 years
At 15 percent, how long will it take to double your money? 72 ÷ 15 = 4.8 years

The Rule of 72 can also be used to calculate what compound growth or interest rate you need to double your money in a chosen number of years.

Examples:

To double your money in four years: 72 ÷ 4 = 18 percent interest is required.

To double your money in eight years: 72 ÷ 8 = 9 percent interest is required.

SAVING

There are a number of ways of going about achieving your savings plan:

'TIME-BASED' SAVINGS PLAN

With a time-based savings plan you aim at achieving your goal by a certain date. You therefore calculate how much money you will have to save every month to achieve your goal. For example, say you want to buy a motor car in three years' time for R18 000. You would have to save R500 a month. For the purpose of this calculation, I have left out any interest you would be earning on your savings – but I have also left out the effect of inflation on your savings. Remember that the car that R18 000 will buy you today is not the same one you will buy in three years' time for the same amount of money. Inflation will have pushed that R18 000 up.

'PERCENTAGE OF EARNINGS' SAVINGS PLAN

With this system you work out how much of the money you receive each month you can afford to save. So, say you decide on an amount of 10 percent of your income and your income is R2 000 a month. You will save R2 400 a year – but remember that your income normally increases every year. If your income goes up by more than the inflation rate, then you are getting a real increase in your income. If you use this method of saving, you will then be able to work out at which date you will reach your savings goal.

UNDERSTANDING INFLATION

If compound interest is your friend, inflation is your biggest enemy. Inflation means a general and sustained increase in prices of products and services over fixed periods. Inflation can be caused by a number of things. There are two main causes:

- **Push inflation:** For example, if the price of petrol goes up, it affects a wide range of product producers, forcing them to push up prices at which they sell goods to you. Increases in salaries and wages can have the same effect.

- **Pull inflation:** This happens when there is too much money around and too few products. This means that producers can charge more for their products. This situation is often caused by people borrowing too much money to spend on consumer goods, particularly luxuries.

Inflation not only affects the prices of goods and services, but can also have an impact on your savings.

As a general rule, when you save money you should work on your money growing by what is called a 'real rate' of growth. This takes account of inflation. A real rate of return is calculated by subtracting the inflation rate from the interest rate you are earning.

Example: If the interest rate your bank gives you is 15 percent, but the inflation rate is 10 percent, then you are actually receiving 5 percent a year. When you start paying income tax, you also need to include this in your calculations in order to establish your real rate of interest. You pay tax on interest you earn. There is an initial amount of interest that is tax free to encourage you to save. In 2002, the tax-free amount for people under the age of 65 was R6 000 a year.

DIFFERENT INTEREST RATES

There are two types of interest rates:

Simple interest: With simple interest you are quoted one rate for the period of your investment.

Compound interest: Here you will be paid interest on interest. Interest can be added to your savings every month, three months, six months or annually. Compound interest is obviously better than simple interest.

There are two ways of being told about interest rates – there are so-called nominal rates, and there are effective rates.

Nominal rates: These are the rates that are quoted for one year. For example, 10 percent on R1 000 would give you R100 a year in interest, but while you are quoted the nominal rate you will find that you are actually being paid (if you have invested money) or are paying (if you have borrowed money) compound interest. This means that you are paying or receiving more than the nominal rate you have been quoted.

Effective rates: If your interest is paid to you more than once a year and the interest is added to your investment, you will receive a larger amount of interest. For example, say you invest R1 000 for a year at a nominal rate of 10 percent, but the interest is credited to you every six months:

Investment:	R1 000
Six months' interest:	R50 (R100 ÷ 2)
Subtotal:	R1 050
Next six months' interest:	R52.50
Total investment value:	R1 102.50

So, by receiving interest every six months, you have received an extra R2.50. Your nominal rate was 10 percent a year, but your effective rate was 10.25 percent a year.

It is important to find out whether you are being quoted an effective or nominal rate. Many institutions quote you an effective rate when you invest money, but quote you the nominal rate when you borrow money from them. This can be very misleading.

Always work in effective interest rates. It is more accurate.

WHEN TO START SAVING

The sooner you start saving, the easier you will get into the habit of saving. The difficult thing is to start. It is always easier to start saving when you have a target or a savings goal. Unfortunately, nowadays it is quite easy to borrow money. This makes what is called 'instant gratification' much easier, but there is a price to pay. If you borrow money to pay for something, in the end you pay very much more than you would have paid if you had paid cash. Firstly, you pay the interest on your borrowings. Secondly, when you pay cash you can often get a discount.

The result of borrowing is that in the end you actually own far less, and you have the worry of debt repayments.

Next let's look at where you put your savings.

BANKING

Banks are about the best place to keep your savings until you start investing your money. You can open your own bank account at most banks from the age of seven. Most banks offer different types of bank accounts for different age groups. Until the age of 18 you will, in most cases, only be able to operate a savings account. You will earn interest, but there may also be charges. You must shop around and compare the costs and interest you will receive using a bank savings account.

Here is a list you can use to make comparisons between banks:

Service	Absa	FNB	Nedbank	Standard	Other
Account name					
Interest rate					
Minimum balance					
Charge for using own ATM					
Charge for using other ATMs					
Other transaction charges					
Monthly charge					
Deposit charge					
Cash deposit charge					
Any other charges					
Number of withdrawals allowed					

AUTOMATED TELLER MACHINES

Nearly all bank accounts operate with automated teller machine (ATM) cards, which allow you to make deposits and withdrawals and to check your balance. ATMs can be very useful, but you must be aware of the dangers.

You must be very careful when using an ATM, because they have become the targets of crooks that are out to steal your money. Here are some rules you should follow:

- Place a limit on the amount of money that can be withdrawn from your account in any one day. You can do this yourself at the ATM. If there is an emergency and you need more money, all you have to do is go to a bank branch with your ID book and savings card. The bank officials will make an arrangement for you to withdraw extra money.

- If someone asks you for help at an ATM, decline politely and refer them to the bank. Often when people ask for help they use it as a ruse to switch ATM cards and clean out your account.
- If your card appears to be jammed, telephone your bank immediately and have the card cancelled. The banks all have emergency telephone numbers. Crooks often create a blockage in ATM machines to steal your card as soon as you leave.
- Do not use ATMs at any time they appear to be isolated with few people around. Rather find another ATM. This is particularly the case at night and over weekends.
- Do not let anyone see you entering your code. If you are feeling crowded, ask the person or people to stand back, or leave and come back later. Also be aware that someone may be watching you through binoculars from a distance in an attempt to get your PIN code.
- If you are at all suspicious of anything, delay doing the transaction.
- Always remember to remove your cash, your card and your transaction record.
- Do not keep your PIN code in the same place as your ATM card, and definitely do not write it on your card. It is best to memorise your code and leave the record of it in a safe place at home.
- Finally, if you are threatened at an ATM, rather let the people have the money. It is better than being injured, or worse. However, try to memorise what the people look like. Immediately report any incident to the police and to your bank.

MOVING UP THE BANKING LADDER

When you find that you have to pay accounts, for example for rent, electricity or the telephone, you may find that a savings account is no longer adequate. It can be dangerous to walk around with large amounts of money in your pocket, and you are equally at risk if you send cash in the mail.

When you start controlling quite a lot of money and you have a fair number of transactions every week, it is best to have two accounts: one where you can keep your money that you use for everyday expenses and spending, and another in which you keep your savings. In that way you will be less tempted to draw on your savings, particularly if you keep your savings bank card in a safe place at home. You can have the bank link your two accounts, which can be useful. Say you have your allowance or anything you earn paid into your 'daily use' savings account, you can use the ATM to transfer a percentage to your 'savings' savings account.

As you earn more and your financial transactions become more compli-cated, you will find that banks offer a vast array of services. They offer numerous different types of bank accounts that you can use to save or borrow money, as well as many other services to help you keep your personal and business finances in order. You must accept that the more services a bank offers you, the more you will have to pay. So, do not step up the level of service that you get just so that you can look important by having a cheque account.

TRANSMISSION ACCOUNT

Most banks offer what are called transmission accounts. These accounts are useful when you start having to do at least 10 to 20 transactions every month. A transmission account is a type of savings account, but you are also able to make a limited number of cheque payments every month and have regular amounts deducted (stop orders or debit orders) to pay other people or businesses. The cheques can either be obtained through special bank ATMs or through what are called call centres, where you give an instruction over the telephone for someone to be sent a cheque. You can open a transmission account as a teenager without any problem, because you have no option but to keep the account in a credit balance. In other words, some of your money is always in the account. ATMs are programmed so that you cannot withdraw more money than you have in the account. You therefore cannot go into a debit balance where you would owe the bank money.

You should understand the difference between a stop order and a debit order.

A **stop order** is an instruction that you give to your bank to pay a regular amount to another party by way of a deduction from your account. You can stop or alter a stop order at will.

A **debit order** is an instruction you give to another party allowing them to remove money from your account. For example, you could agree to let a unit trust company deduct a certain amount from your account every month as part of your investment plan. However, you must be aware that debit orders can be dangerous and are often abused by scam artists. You should not sign a debit order with just any party. You should restrict debit orders to reputable companies. You should also place a limit on the amount of money that may be debited, and fill in the date on which the debit order can be effected. You should check that the correct amount is deducted every month and that double deductions are not made. When you cancel a debit order you must cancel it with the party with which you have the agreement, not with the bank. If a debit order is deducted from your account that you have not authorised, you must inform your bank immediately and they will reverse the entry. It is, however, virtually impossible to get the bank to cancel the debit order permanently. You may have to close your account in extreme circumstances.

CHEQUE ACCOUNT (ALSO KNOWN AS A CURRENT ACCOUNT)

Here the number of facilities increases again. You can make out limitless numbers of cheques. The most important difference is that you can also be given loans – called overdrafts – by your bank through a cheque account. Cheque accounts come with numerous options. You can have accounts where you are paid interest on your money; others where there is a guarantee to anyone accepting your cheque that the bank will definitely pay up; and yet others where if you keep a minimum balance you don't pay bank charges. You need to compare the costs to see what is right for you. Don't try to show off by getting a special account that implies you have special status. The account will cost you more and you may not need the special services that come with it.

Normally you have to be 21 to open a cheque account. However, banks will consider opening a cheque account for you from the age of 16 under special conditions. These are:

- You will need the consent of your parents or legal guardian;
- You will have to show why you need a current account;
- You will have to prove that you are a responsible person who handles money properly;
- You will not be allowed to go into a debit balance (overdraft) unless there are very special circumstances; and
- If the bank did agree to let you go into overdraft, it would want your parents or guardian to stand surety. This means that your parents or guardian would have to sign a legal agreement to repay any money you owe to the bank if you are unable to do so yourself.

Filling in a cheque

A cheque can be exactly like cash, but cheques are often used fraudulently. It is important to look after a chequebook and to fill in a cheque correctly.

As a general rule you should avoid making out cheques for cash, as a cheque can change hands many times and open you up to fraud. To ensure your safety you should follow these steps:

- Always use a pen, and not a pencil, to fill out a cheque.
- Fill in the full name of the person or the institution you are making the payment to, and draw a double line through any unused space. You should avoid using abbreviated names, such as SARS for the South African Revenue Service. A fraudster can change SARS to SARS Smith. By drawing lines through the remaining space you also prevent the name of the person being altered.
- Cross out the phrase 'or bearer'. If this remains, it means the person to whom you gave the cheque can endorse it to someone else.
- You must fill in the amount both in figures and in numerals. Again draw double lines through any unused space to prevent figures being altered.
- Fill in the date. You can fill in a date in advance. This is called a post-dated cheque, and the bank will not deduct the amount from your account until that date.
- Write clearly across the top of the cheque 'Not Transferable'. This means the cheque may only be paid into the account of the person or institution named on the cheque.
- Fill in the stub so that you have a record of how much was paid, to whom and when.
- If you make a mistake, write 'cancelled' on the cheque and stub. Banks will not accept altered cheques.

CREDIT CARDS

These cards are exactly what they say they are. They are a banking facility that allows you to pay for just about anything without actually needing to have any cash. Every month you are sent an account, which you must pay in full, or else you will be charged a very high rate of interest. You can, however, also keep money in your credit card account, on which you will earn interest. Credit cards are definitely not for people who find it easy to spend money they do not have. Banks do not easily issue credit cards to people under the age of 21. If they do, they will require an undertaking from your parents that they will pay up if you do not pay what is due.

ELECTRONIC BANKING

Banks know that they have to become more efficient to cut down on costs and to make it easier for us, their customers, to do our banking. A major expense for banks is all the branches they have around the country. They are also an irritation for us, as we have to stand in queues. So, banks now encourage us to do our banking from a distance.

The first step was ATM machines. This was followed by telephone call centres, which allow you to telephone your bank and give it instructions.

Bank customers with transmission or current accounts use call centres. When you call you are required to give certain codes so that the bank official knows you are who you say you are. Once you have been cleared you can give instructions for payments or other transactions to be made. With a call centre you do not even have to use a chequebook, as the money is transferred electronically from your account to the account of the person or business you have to pay.

The third electronic step, which most banks have now introduced for most customers, is Internet banking, where you access your bank account on your computer and give instructions for payments, check your balance and get statements. This is the banking of the future. Big bank halls and branches all over the place will soon become history.

KEEPING ON THE RIGHT SIDE OF YOUR BANK

When you operate a bank account you must do it in a responsible way. This is particularly the case with a cheque account. With a cheque account it is possible to issue a cheque without any money in your account. If you do this without the permission of your bank manager it is illegal, and technically you could be sent to jail. Not only will the person to whom you gave the cheque be fed up, but so will the bank. The bank will not pay up. It will charge you a hefty fee for sending the cheque back to the person who deposited it, and if you persist in issuing 'dud' cheques your account will be closed and you will find it difficult to get banking facilities elsewhere. If you need to 'overdraw' your bank account – in effect borrow money from the bank – you must speak to the bank manager first. The bank manager will arrange to give you an overdraft through which you can borrow the money – if you are considered to be a responsible customer. Remember, you will be charged interest on the money you borrow.

4

Investing

Investment is one step up from saving. It is not merely about putting money in a bank; it is about using a wide variety of different financial instruments to make money for you. A financial instrument is any type of investment. The major difference between saving and investing is that now you are going to take risks with your savings. So, before you move into the wider world of investments, you must understand the risks involved.

Saving your money in a bank account is a form of investing, because you are earning interest on the amount you have saved. However, banking is a low-risk form of investing because the bank guarantees it will pay back your capital (the amount you saved) plus the interest at the rate it promised to pay. Because you have all these guarantees, you would normally not expect to get a high return (interest rate) on your money. In many cases the return is below the inflation rate, so you are losing rather than making money.

There are three basic ways that you can earn money on your savings. These are:

- **Interest and rent:** This is a fixed amount that is paid for money you invest.
- **Dividends:** This is the share of profit that is paid to owners (shareholders) of a company.
- **Capital growth:** Capital is the money you invest. Capital growth is the profit you can make by buying something cheaply and then selling it at a higher price. If you buy something for more than the price at which you sell, you will make a capital loss.

There are two basic types of investments that provide one or more ways of growing your investments. These are:

- **Lending investments:** These are investments where you lend money to your bank (an interest-earning savings account) or a bond (for example, where you lend money to the government).
- **Ownership investments:** These include property or shares in companies.

INVESTMENT RISK

Most investments centre on the risk you will take in losing all your money and/or not getting a return (growth) on your investment that outstrips the inflation rate. With a high-risk investment, it is possible for you to lose everything. With a low-risk investment, you may lose nothing or only a very small portion of your investment.

The first step in assessing risk is to look at what are called financial asset classes. Asset classes are a way of separating different investments into groupings that reflect mainly what type of investments they are, the type of returns you can expect and the risk involved. Here is a table of the main asset classes and the level of risk:

Asset Class	Examples	Level of Risk
Cash	Bank savings, deposit accounts and money market	Low
Property	Houses or business properties	Low to medium
Bonds (gilts)	Loans made to government and companies	Medium
Shares (equities)	Companies listed on a stock exchange	Medium to high
	Companies not listed on a stock exchange	High

WHAT IS A CASH INVESTMENT?

Cash investments are mainly used for when you do not want to tie up your money for lengthy periods, or you are in the process of building up sufficient money to buy a longer-term investment, such as property. A cash investment covers a number of different areas. The most common is a bank savings account, but there are many more. Cash investments are those where interest only is paid on your money. Other cash investments include:

- **Term deposits:** These are also called fixed deposits. You lend a bank money for a fixed period of time at a fixed interest rate, normally for a period of between three months and three years.
- **Money market:** Money market investments are offered by unit trust companies and banks. Your money is pooled together with other small investors and lent to big institutions. This way you get a higher interest rate. You are also usually able to withdraw your money with 48 hours' notice. However, you need at least R20 000 as a minimum investment amount.
- **Notional certificates of deposit (NCDs):** These are fairly substantial amounts of money lent to large institutions such as banks and businesses, usually for a period of three months.

WHAT IS A PROPERTY INVESTMENT?

A property investment can be a lot more than buying your own home. There are plenty of different types of investment in property. The main reason why people invest in property is to get capital growth, but you can also receive rental income. Property investments, which mainly require substantial amounts of money, include:

- **Residential property**, where you own a property but someone else pays you rent to live there;
- **Commercial or industrial property**, where you own the property and a business pays you rent;
- **Mortgage participation bonds**, where you lend money to someone else to buy property;
- **Life assurance endowment policies**, which have their underlying investments in property;
- **Property unit trusts**, where you can invest smaller amounts of money in companies that specialise in investing in property; and

- **Property syndications**, where you form a 'syndicate' with a number of other people to purchase a property.

WHAT ARE BOND INVESTMENTS?

A bond (also known as gilts because the certificates used to be edged with gold foil) is simply another way of saying you are lending money to a big institution, such as the government. Bonds are certificates that are issued when big institutions such as the government, your local municipality, Telkom, Eskom or a large company want to borrow money. They borrow your money and pay you interest.

After bonds have been issued (in what is called the primary market), many investors buy and sell them (the secondary market, called a bond market) depending on where they see interest rates going in the future. Bonds are strange things in that when interest rates are high, no one wants to invest in them. Government has to offer high interest rates to attract investors to lend it money. This means you can buy a bond cheaply. When interest rates are low, a lot of investors want to buy them, so the bonds become expensive.

As a result you can make money from the interest that is paid as well as the price of the bonds. If you bought the bond cheaply and sold it when it was expensive, you would make what is called a capital gain. In other words, your original investment (your capital) became worth more.

If you invested in bonds when they were expensive and sold them when they became cheap, you would suffer a capital loss.

The bond market is very complex, and bond traders spend many years gaining experience in dealing in bonds. The bond market is also referred to as the capital market.

WHAT ARE SHARES?

When you buy a share (an equity), you are buying a part or a share in a company. You become a part owner. As a part owner you expect to get part of the profits. If a company had 10 shares and you bought one share you could expect to get one-tenth of the profits. When profits are paid out to shareholders (people who own shares) the payment is called a dividend.

Companies sell shares when they want additional money to expand, or buy new machinery, or buy another company.

Once they have sold the shares to investors, the investors also buy and sell shares. There are a number of reasons why a shareholder may not want to hold on to the shares he or she owns. They may need the money for something else; or they do not like the way the company is being managed and feel that profits will drop; or the company is out of date (for example, it may still be making typewriters, which no one wants to buy, instead of computers).

The price of a share will go up or down depending on what investors think about the future profits of the company. If they think a company is going to make great profits, a lot of investors will want to buy the share, so the price of the share will go up.

So, as with bonds, you can also make a capital gain (if you bought the share when it was cheap and sold it when it went up in price), but again you can make a capital loss because shares can also come down in value. If share markets are generally following an upward trend, it is known as a 'Bull Market'. If share markets are generally falling, it is known as a 'Bear Market'.

You can purchase listed shares on stock markets around the world (the JSE Securities Exchange in South Africa), or unlisted shares in private deals in companies that are not listed on an exchange. You have far more security with listed shares.

A share market is also known as an equity market.

HOW TO START INVESTING?

For many people, particularly when you are young, it is difficult to know where to start investing. Most investments require minimum amounts that are quite large, and when you put all your money into, say, the shares of a single company, the risk is high.

The first thing to consider is how to reduce the risk of losing your money when investing. There are 10 rules that you must always follow when investing:

Rule 1: Don't be rushed. Never be rushed into making an investment decision. There are many opportunities available and missing one will not undermine your wealth.

Rule 2: A long-term affair. Investment is a long-term affair, particularly in shares and bonds. Over the long term, investments in bonds and stock market listed shares have always given an above-inflation return. If you invest for the short term in bonds and shares you can lose money for two reasons. The first is that you will not have given your investments sufficient time to recover the investment costs; and second, investment markets move up and down. This is known as volatility. If you need to sell in the short term, the markets may be down and you will lose money. Once you have made a commitment you should stick with it for a lengthy period of at least five years, but preferably for 10 years or more.

Rule 3: Investigate. Never invest in something merely because your neighbour or your hairdresser says they have made money from something. Investigate carefully before you invest in anything. You can use facilities such as the Internet, your bank or a financial adviser. You should always check that an investment is legal. The best way to establish this is by contacting the Financial Services Board (www.fsb.co.za).

Rule 4: Never believe the extraordinary. If someone offers you an investment with, say, a 30 percent or higher return a year, the chances are that you are being had. This is not to say that there are not safe investments that do at times make very high returns. The issue is whether someone can safely predict that such high returns can be made on a consistent basis. No one can, and if they could they are hardly likely to share this wisdom with you.

Rule 5: Be consistent. Don't switch between investments. Every time you do, you are giving away part of your money in additional costs.

Rule 6: Don't panic. When markets go down or someone tells you that they are getting a better return elsewhere, don't panic. Markets go up and down. If you have made a sound decision initially, stick it out. Study after study shows that many investors panic when markets fall and sell their investments, and then buy back in when prices are high. If you have made a decision that you want your money in five years' time and there is a market crash after one year, all you have suffered is what is called a paper loss. In other words, on paper your capital may be worth less, but because you are not withdrawing your investment you have not suffered any actual loss.

Rule 7: Don't borrow to invest. Borrowing to invest is highly dangerous. To invest by borrowing is a high-risk strategy and requires sound investment knowledge.

Rule 8: Don't believe predictions. Don't believe people who say that they can predict what will happen in the share market. If they really knew on which date the share market would start shooting up, do you think they would tell you? If you jump in and out of investments you are not an investor any more; you become a speculator, which is a polite way of saying you are a gambler.

Rule 9: Ask dumb questions. First of all, your questions will not be dumb. It is your money and you should ask as many questions as you want about all aspects of an investment. Among the questions you should ask (and get replies in writing) are:

- What are the costs, both initial and annual? Total costs, including commissions paid to financial intermediaries, above 6.5 percent for initial costs and 2 percent for annual costs, are too high.
- What commissions are paid, both initial and annual? Payments to financial advisers should not be more than 3 percent as the initial commission, and 0.5 percent for annual commission. An annual commission should only be paid if you are receiving regular advice. You can negotiate commissions.
- What is the investment period?
- What are the underlying investments, for example are they shares, bonds or something else?
- How often will you receive reports on your investment?
- Are there any guarantees on capital and/or on growth?
- What has been the investment return on the investment for the past five years?
- What are the tax consequences?
- What is the name of the company marketing the investment?
- What is the track record of the company doing the investment?
- What risks are involved?

If you cannot get satisfactory replies or the salesperson patronises you, walk away.

Rule 10: Diversify your investments. This is another way of saying, 'Don't put all your eggs in one basket.' If you have a number of different investments in asset classes and in different sections of asset classes (e.g. more than one company in equities) you are not likely to lose all your money, as one investment will normally be performing.

Diversification can be a problem

Very few ordinary people invest directly in bonds and shares for three main reasons. These are:

- You need quite large amounts of money to buy a single investment in bonds or shares in a company;
- Very few people have the time to research all the different companies and bonds; and
- You need to buy quite a lot of investments to be able to diversify properly.

The solution is in collective/ pooled investments

With collective (pooled) investments, your money and the money of many other smaller investors are pooled together. This enables the company managing the pooled investment to invest your money across asset classes and within a variety of choices within the asset classes. In effect, you can have the same investment portfolio as South Africa's space traveller and technology billionaire, Mark Shuttleworth. The only difference is that you will have smaller portions invested in each underlying investment, such as a variety of company shares.

Pooled investments answer many of our problems about risk

- Diversification: You buy into lots of companies, thus reducing the risk of having all your money in a single investment (i.e. a single company).
- Research: Pooled investment companies pay analysts who study investment opportunities.
- Reduce risk: Generally, pooled investments are strictly controlled by law, and it is unlikely that your money will be stolen.

The big benefit of pooled investments is that you invest smaller amounts of money on a regular basis. Some pooled investment companies will let you invest as little as R100 a month.

Pooled investments are available in two main forms. These are:

- Unit trust funds (called mutual funds internationally).
- Life assurance endowment policies.

It is best to start with balanced or general equity funds.

Pooled investments offer you a variety of choices that can widen or narrow the diversification of your investments, and with it the risk profile. You can select from a wide range, starting with what are called balanced, managed or asset allocation investments that invest across all asset classes; to investments that only invest in a particular asset class, such as the share market; to a section of an asset class, such as financial services companies. As you learn more about investments, you can consider moving into more narrow fields. But remember, the narrower and less diversified an investment, the more volatile it is likely to be and the greater the chance of losing money.

UNIT TRUST FUNDS

Unit trust funds come in many different forms. Most people invest in what are called general equity funds. General equity funds invest in a wide range of share companies listed on stock exchanges in South Africa and, more recently, overseas as well.

But other unit trust funds specialise in different sections of the investment markets. There are some, for example, that only invest in gold mines; others may only invest in small companies; while you even have some funds, called ethical funds, which will not invest in companies that make booze or that do not treat their employees fairly.

These more narrowly focused funds usually have a greater degree of risk because they are not as well diversified as a general equity fund. There are two main divisions of unit trust funds. These are:

- **Income funds:** These funds are structured to give you an income. They make investments where interest is paid. These investments are mainly in bonds and cash deposits. Income funds are used mainly by people who need an income, such as pensioners.
- **Capital growth funds:** These funds look for investments where the value of your capital improves because the value of investments, such as shares, grows.

HOW TO INVEST IN UNIT TRUSTS

There are a number of ways to invest in unit trusts:

- You can speak to a financial adviser, who will also give you advice;
- You can speak to your bank; or
- You can contact a unit trust company directly.

A big advantage of unit trust investments is that you can invest and withdraw whenever you want.

Lump-sum or monthly investments: You can make lump-sum investments (also known as single premium) or monthly investments (also called recurring premium). If you have taken the recurring premium route and you are short of money one month, you can stop paying in without any penalty. If you find you have extra money you can also pay it in. However, you should not treat your unit trust investment like a savings account, where you can deposit and withdraw small amounts on an ongoing basis. You should see investing in unit trust funds as a medium- to long-term investment with the absolute minimum period being five years. The reason for this is that you have to give the investment markets time to work in your favour (they mainly go up erratically), and to work out the costs. The only exception is if you have your money in a money market fund, where costs are lower and your return is determined by interest rates.

Minimum investments: Different unit trust funds have different minimum investment amounts. These can range from R100 to R2 000 a month for recurring premium investments, and from R500 to R20 000 for single premium investments. General equity funds normally have lower minimum premiums.

There are costs involved in investing in unit trusts. These include:

Initial cost: You are normally charged up to 7 percent of the value of your investment when you make the investment. So, if you invest R100 of this amount, you would have R93 invested. Of this 7 percent, up to 3 percent goes towards paying commission to financial advisers, 2 percent goes to the unit trust management company to pay for its administration costs and its profits, and the rest goes to pay tax and the stockbrokers who buy and sell shares on behalf of the unit trust fund.

Annual cost: Every year another amount is deducted to cover the costs of all the experts who are used to manage your money. This is known as the annual asset management fee. Until 1998, unit trust management companies were only permitted to charge you one percent of the value of your capital (the value of your investment) each year. Now they can charge you anything. What happens is that high-performing funds normally cost more. You must always check how much you are going to be charged, as this can make a big difference to the performance you get from your investment.

UNIT TRUST FUND CHOICES

Unit trust funds are divided into different categories. The reason for this is so that you can quickly work out things such as investment diversification and the potential risk of each fund. Here is a list of the different unit trust fund categories, a description of what they do and their risk:

Income funds (low risk): Income funds provide income to investors. Income funds put your money into cash investments, such as short-term loans to financial institutions, and into bonds.

Money market funds (low risk): Money market funds are similar investments to income funds, but their purpose is for investors with large amounts of money, who are concerned about the risks of investing in the stock market or who need the money in the near future, to get a good return on their money while making up their minds. The advantage of a money market fund over a bank fixed deposit is that you can withdraw your money at short notice. Another use of a money market fund is for phasing large lump sums into other investments. Say you inherited a large sum of money – the best strategy is to buy shares or unit trusts gradually so that you even out the ups and downs of investment markets. You would put most of the money into the money market fund and gradually phase it into other investments.

Managed prudential funds (low to medium risk): These funds are for money invested in retirement savings. By law, retirement investments can only have 75 percent invested in shares. The rest must be invested in bonds, cash or property. The reason for this is to reduce risk. You do not want to take big risks with retirement fund money.

Managed flexible funds (medium risk): These funds are similar to managed prudential funds in that they invest in cash, bonds and shares, but the fund manager can invest any amount in any of the three asset classes. With these funds you are asking the fund manager to make the choice of asset class as well as the underlying investments, such as which shares to select in the share market. These are quite good funds for first-time investors.

Bond (gilt) funds (low to medium risk): Most of the money is invested in bonds, but also in cash.

Fund of funds (low to high risk): Also known as multi-manager funds, funds of funds invest in other unit trust funds, bringing together different combinations. A fund of funds will describe what it is trying to achieve. The cost of investing in multi-manager funds of any type, unit trust or life assurance investment products, tends to be higher, as there is another level of management cost added. The argument given in favour of a multi-manager investment is that the best managers (experts in different sectors) from all asset manager companies can be chosen.

Index funds (medium to high risk): The way that most people judge how particular investments are doing is by comparing the investments with particular indexes. There are a large number of indexes. The most well known is the JSE Securities Exchange All Share Index. The index is put together by people who are very good at mathematics and statistics (actuaries). They take into account factors such as how much the total value of the shares of each company listed on the stock exchange is worth, and how that compares to the total value of all the shares of all the companies on the JSE. There are indexes for different sections of the JSE, such as gold shares, industrial shares, financial services companies, bonds and even the top 40 most valuable companies (the ALSI40). Index unit trust funds match the same proportions of shares as those in an index. The name of the fund will always describe the name of the index selected. Index funds are very popular overseas, as very few fund managers are able to consistently outperform selected indexes. As investing in an index fund requires little skill from a fund manager your costs should be lower.

General equity funds (medium risk): General equity funds invest in the broad range of shares available. The fund manager may also keep a large amount of money in cash if there is concern that shares are overvalued. You should always check the cash proportion as you may have a different belief from the fund manager. You may want to be what is called 'fully invested'. This means that you want all your money invested in shares. General equity funds are also a good choice for first-time investors.

International funds (medium risk): These funds make investments in foreign companies and bonds. They can be similar to general equity funds, managed funds and bond funds, except that most of the investments are made overseas. You need to check on each fund to see what investments it makes. It is a good thing to have some of your money invested overseas as it helps to diversify your risk, particularly when the rand is losing its value against other major currencies. So, if the rand loses 30 percent of its value against the US dollar, as it did in 1998, you have already made 30 percent on your investment.

Industrial funds (medium to high risk): Industrial funds only invest in industrial companies listed on the Johannesburg Stock Exchange. Because they only invest in a certain section, your risk is increased because there is less diversification.

Specific equity funds (medium to high risk): Specific equity funds make investments in selected sectors of a stock exchange or in what are called themes. So-called ethical or socially responsible funds fall into this category because they only invest in, say, companies that do not wreck the environment.

Small companies funds (medium to high risk): Small companies are often considered to be the best place to invest because they can make rapid changes and take advantage of opportunities quickly. The managers have normally started the company and are prepared to work very hard to make it a success. These companies are often involved in taking on the big companies in profitable areas, known as niches. In 1997, unit trust funds investing in this sector were among the best-performing unit trusts and became very popular with investors, but a lot of people lost a lot of money when the sector collapsed a year later. They forgot the golden rule of diversifying their investments.

Mining and resource funds (high risk): These funds are also a type of commodity fund, because the companies in which the funds invest produce materials used to manufacture other goods. All commodity investments are what are called cyclical investments (the shares go up or down following cycles in the economy). For example, if there is solid economic growth around the world, then motor car manufacturers will be selling lots of cars. This means a higher demand for materials used in making cars, such as steel. This in turn means that steel manufacturers need additional materials, such as iron, manganese and coal, which in turn should push up the prices of those commodities. But when economic conditions are depressed the shares will lose value, as fewer motor cars will be manufactured.

Gold funds (high risk): Gold used to be the most important export of South Africa, but the value of gold has lost favour for a number of reasons:

- At one stage all the world's money was backed by gold. For every note of money there was gold backing it up. This is no longer the case, although many central banks of various countries hold gold as reserves. (A country's reserves are its savings to pay for such things as imports.)
- In times of war and economic disruption, gold used to be considered the currency of last reserve. This meant that gold would always retain its value, and you would be able to flee to another country taking your assets with you. The currency of the country in which you lived could have become worthless anywhere else in the world, but gold would retain its value. Nowadays the US dollar is considered the currency of last reserve. Gold has dropped dramatically in price, but profits can still be made from gold. It is about the riskiest unit trust investment you can make in formal investment markets.

INVESTMENT STYLES

In equity unit trust funds (funds that invest in shares) you will find themes in the way fund managers choose shares. Here are four main themes or styles of selecting shares:

Top down: The fund manager looks at what the whole economy is likely to do. If the expectation is that the economy is doing well – and certain sectors of the economy will do better than others (for example, the government will start building lots of houses for the poor) – then companies will be selected that will benefit (for example, cement, brick and steel-manufacturing companies should do well). Top-down managers will often look for what are called cyclical shares. These are shares that perform better or worse depending on how different parts of the economy are doing. The opposite of a cyclical share is a defensive share. These companies manufacture things such as medicines or food, which people will always buy, so they tend not to be affected by changes in the economy.

Bottom up: Also known as stock picking, a bottom-up fund manager looks for particular companies that should do well for a number of reasons. A stock-picker investment manager looks for companies that have shares that are considered undervalued, or that can be expected to make large profits in the future. Among other things, they will carefully read balance sheets and examine the management of a company.

Value: Here fund managers will look for shares of companies that they consider undervalued or cheap. There are a number of ways to test whether a company is undervalued. One of the most popular ways is to see what the total value of shares of the company is against the total value of everything the company owns (the net asset value or NAV). Say the NAV is worth R50 million, but the total value of shares (the number of shares sold multiplied by the price of the shares) is only worth R40 million, then the company is described as trading at a discount to NAV. It can then be considered a value stock. But say the total value of all the shares of the company is worth R60 million, that is, R10 million more than its NAV, then it would be considered to be trading at a premium to NAV. This means it is not a value stock. There can be many reasons why a company is undervalued. It may be in an industry that is out of favour, it may not have made very good profits, or even shown a loss. Not all undervalued companies need be good bargains. Incidentally, Warren Buffett, whom I mentioned before, one of the world's richest people, is a value investor.

Growth: A growth manager looks for companies that are likely to grow quickly and profits that will also grow quickly. More often than not these companies trade at a premium to NAV. They also usually have what is called a high price-to-earnings (p/e) ratio. This means that the profits made by the company are very low in comparison to the price of the shares. The p/e is calculated by dividing profits by the value of the shares. The lower the p/e ratio, the cheaper the share is in relation to the profits it is expected to make. The higher the p/e, the more expensive the share is in relation to the profit, but investors are obviously prepared to invest in the share because they expect the company to make tremendous profits in the future. A p/e of more than 20 is considered to be high. A p/e also tells you how many years it will take for you to recover the money you have invested. A p/e of 20 means it will take 20 years to receive profits equal to your initial investment.

Not all unit trust funds in the same category invest in the same shares. Fund managers will use different methods, such as value or growth processes, in selecting shares. As a result the risk profiles of various unit trust funds in the same category will be different.

SELECTING THE RIGHT FUND FOR YOU

With the number of unit trust funds increasing almost every week, it is becoming increasingly difficult to select the right investment. There are things you should not do and things you should do when investing in unit trust funds:

WHAT YOU SHOULD NOT DO

- Do not look for the best-performing fund in all categories of that day. The fund could easily become a bottom performer very quickly because the fund manager may be taking big risks in the investments being made.
- Do not invest in a specialist fund if you are a first-time investor and do not know much about unit trust funds.
- Do not select, say, the top three general equity funds because you cannot make up your mind about the right fund. While diversification of invest-ments is a good thing, over-diversification is also dangerous in that you will start to lower your performance.
- Do not invest in a fund merely because your next-door neighbour says it is the best fund. Do some research and try to find out the reasons why it is doing well, or could be doing well.

WHAT YOU SHOULD DO

- You should select a unit trust management company that has a family of funds. A unit trust company family of funds means that it will have a number of different funds in different categories. For example, it will have general equity, specialist, bond, income and money market funds. This will allow you to switch between different funds at low or no cost as you become more sophisticated in unit trust investment.

- Find out about the asset managers. Often the performance of a fund is determined by the team or individual who manages your money. If the team has been around for some time and has been producing good results, this is a good sign. Although many people look for high-flying individual fund managers, there is a danger that they will move to another company, which could cause problems for you and additional expenses. You can ask the fund about its managers, who they are and how long they have been there.
- Look at performance tables of all types. You can judge how your unit trust investments are doing by looking at performance and price tables published in most newspapers. You can calculate how much your unit trust is worth by multiplying the number of units you own by the repurchase price. You can also see how the different funds have performed for different periods. You should not see past performance as any indication of future performance. There are many types of performance tables. Among others, there are performance comparisons that show which funds and which unit trust management companies are providing consistent performance, and others that measure the investment risk taken in getting good investment returns.
- Look at the volatility of funds so that you can see what the chances are of a fund underperforming. Volatility figures are published in most newspapers.
- Look at the costs (you can get these from the companies).
- Look at the minimum investments (you can also get these from the companies).

If you have a computer linked to the Internet, most, if not all, unit trust management companies have websites that will give you lots of details about their funds. They also operate call centres that you can telephone to get more details.

LIFE ASSURANCE INVESTMENTS

Life assurance products can be quite complicated, and you often do not receive as much information as with unit trust investments. For example, there are no comparative tables published of the investment performance of life assurance investments. The most important fact to know about a life assurance investment is that it is contractual. You have to invest for a minimum of five years or longer, depending on your contract. If you stop investing or withdraw the money you have invested, you can lose all or part of your money. The contractual nature of the investment has the advantage of making you a disciplined saver, but you do not have the freedom of choice you have with a unit trust investment. Life assurance products mainly divide into two types. These are:

- **Risk assurance:** This means the life assurance company is prepared to take a bet with you. Every month you give it money in case you are badly injured, become very ill, or die. If any of these things happen to you, the life assurance company pays up. This type of assurance is essential if you have people depending on you to survive. It is an investment for the people who depend on you financially.
- **Investment assurance:** Here you are given two main choices:
  - Market-linked or market-related investments, which work very much like unit trusts. Your investment goes up or down in line with the investments made with your money and the money of other people (policyholders). Increasingly, life assurance companies are providing the same investment choices as in unit trusts.
  - Guaranteed investments: These investments come under a number of names, including smoothed bonus and stable bonus. They all do more or less the same thing. In most cases, your capital (your original investment) and growth of about 4 percent are guaranteed. Every year bonuses are declared, which are added to your investment. These investments are particularly attractive for people who do not want to take risks. However, the growth in your investment is not likely to be as good as in a market-linked investment.

OTHER INVESTMENTS

There are many different types of investments, some of which are very safe, but there are others that are merely scams. South Africans repeatedly fall victim to scams because they get greedy – all they see is the promise of large profits and they do not ask the right questions.

Two danger areas:

- Avoid what are called pyramid companies or revolving money schemes. In simple terms, you buy into the scheme and the people ahead of you all get a cut of your money. You are then expected to recruit other people, who in turn will pay in money. You then get a share of their money and a share of the money of people recruited by the people you recruited. These schemes come in many different forms. Many of them are honestly run, but the schemes do attract a large number of crooks that take the money and run. These schemes are not investments, despite what their supporters attempt to tell you – they are a big gamble and you are highly unlikely to get rich by participating in them.

- Unlisted companies. An unlisted company is one that is not listed on a formal stock exchange such as the JSE Securities Exchange. Although such companies are controlled by the Companies Act, they are wide open to abuse. If you are attracted to an investment in an unlisted company, you must do extensive homework before handing over your money. It is usually with unlisted companies that promises of fantastic returns are made, normally with the lure that the company will shortly list on a stock exchange.

5

Don't Do Debt

In your financial affairs, debt is Public Enemy Number One. The single biggest financial problem people have is debt – and you only get into debt in one way: you borrow money you should not borrow, often to buy things you do not really need. Debt can be the cause of many problems, including the break-up of friendships and marriages; great stress and mental breakdowns; loss of your job; theft and imprisonment, sometimes leading to suicide; and, in some very rare circumstances, murder.

Learn the Lesson Now

As a teenager you are unlikely to be able to run up much debt because, if you are given credit (a loan) by a shop to buy, say, clothing, or by a bank without the written permission of your parents or legal guardian while you are under the age of 21, and you cannot repay the money, the bank or shop cannot take legal steps to recover the money. As banks and shops cannot legally recover the debt of a teenager, they will seldom give you credit.

This does not mean that you should not learn about debt while you are still a teenager. There will be times when you need to borrow money. There actually is good debt, but most debt is bad debt.

As you get older and start working, you will find that everyone wants to lend you money. Your bank wants to lend you money, your clothing shop wants to lend you money, motor car dealers want to lend you money, furniture dealers want to give you credit. Open any newspaper and you will always find advertisements offering to sell you something on credit.

You may well ask, if debt is so bad, why is everyone trying to get you into debt? There are two main reasons for this. These are:

- **Interest:** You must pay interest on any money you borrow. Interest is another word for paying rent for using someone else's money. Sometimes this interest can be extremely high. Banks and other institutions make money by lending you money. They borrow money from investors at one interest rate and lend it to you at a higher rate. The difference between the borrowing and lending interest rates is called the spread or the margin, from which banks make their profits.

- **Capture:** Shops in particular want to capture you as a client. They make debt out to be a virtue and that all your desires can be fulfilled by paying 'very little' a month. All sorts of tricks are used to entice you to open an account. An account is just another word for debt (to the store). For example, the store will tell you that you can have R100 free if you open an account and spend R250 on the account. They will also give you a credit limit, which is another way of saying how much debt you will be allowed to build up. And then comes the best part: the store tells you that you need only pay back R50 a month. If you accept all this, have they only got you captured! The store is giving you nothing for free – all it is doing is capturing you as an interest-paying client. By the time you have finished paying back the debt you owe, you will have paid back substantially more than you would have paid if you had paid cash for your purchases. Depending on how long you took to repay the debt, you could find yourself paying double or even triple the original amount.

COMPOUND INTEREST ON DEBT – YOUR ENEMY

In the chapter on saving, it is stated that compound interest is the most important concept you will get from this book. But you also need to remember that compound interest can be your enemy if someone lends you money.

If you borrow R20 000 to buy a car and agree to pay 20 percent a year interest with the loan being repaid over five years, you would pay a total of

R11 792 in interest. And remember, you also have to pay back the R20 000 capital you borrowed. So, the car sold to you for R20 000 finally costs you R31 792. Scary, isn't it!

High debt can cripple any plans you have to save for long-term goals. It can even result in you never owning your own home or being able to make any significant purchase.

GOOD DEBT AND BAD DEBT

There is, however, both good debt and bad debt, and there are ways to identify the two.

Bad debt: Any time you buy something on credit that you can consume, such as food or clothing, or that loses value the moment you buy it, such as furniture or a motor vehicle, that is bad debt. Anything you own that loses value after you have bought it is called a depreciating asset. The reason is that you have lost the value of what you have bought and, if you were in real trouble, you could not sell the items for the same price you paid to get out of debt. If you sold the items you would probably only be able to repay part of the debt.

Good debt: You have good debt when you borrow to buy something for which you do not have the cash, but the item will increase in value. Anything you own that goes up in value after you have bought it is called an appreciating asset. The two best examples are a home and education. Property, over a period of time, mostly does improve in value. So, if you got into financial trouble, you could sell the property and pay off the debt. This does not always happen because property can also lose value, but as a general rule you should be okay.

Borrowing to pay for an education is also good debt. You are investing in yourself to make yourself a sellable commodity. The better educated you are, the more likely you are to make more money, whether you employ yourself by starting your own business, or whether you work for someone else. Education is the most priceless asset you will ever own. It gives you freedom like very little else. Without education you are nearly always trapped in a life where other people make all your decisions.

But you should repay even good debt as quickly as possible. You will save a fortune in interest. Take the example we used earlier to buy a car for

R20 000 over five years at 20 percent interest. To repay the loan over five years you would have to pay R529 a month. If you increased your payments by R100 a month, you would reduce the repayment period by more than a year, and you would save almost R3 000 in interest.

USING DEBT TO MAKE MONEY

There are ways to use debt to make money. In simple terms it works like this: you borrow the money to buy a house. You rent out the house, which pays for the interest you are paying on the loan. In a few years the value of the property has increased. You sell the house and repay the loan. The extra amount you gained is your profit.

Banks and other institutions borrow money from investors so that they can lend it to you at a profit. You can do the same, but it can be dangerous. What happens if you bought a share that is 'guaranteed' to go up, but it crashes in value and you must repay the loan?

This type of borrowing is speculation, which means you are taking a chance that you will make a profit. People who speculate like this try to use words like 'gearing' or 'buying on margin' to make what is generally an unacceptable investment strategy more respectable. When you use debt to speculate you must really know what you are doing. Most often people use debt to speculate in buying property and shares listed on a stock exchange.

SOMETIMES EVEN BAD DEBT IS UNAVOIDABLE

There are times where you cannot avoid bad debt:

- **Bad luck:** For example, you may have a serious car accident that could result in your being unable to work and earn money, cost you a lot in medical bills and require you to spend more on a new car.
- **Necessity:** You may have to buy a car to get to work or to lectures at varsity or tech.
- **Changes in interest rates:** Depending on the agreement you had with the person lending you money, sometimes interest rates go up in line with all other interest rates, way above the original amount at which you borrowed the money, meaning you have to find a lot more money to pay off your debt each month.
- **A once-in-a-lifetime opportunity:** This could be as small a cost as R250 for a ticket to a Robbie Williams concert, or as expensive as

R15 000 for an educational trip to the South Pole to study the mating calls of the Emperor Penguin, but these opportunities tend to be wants rather than essential needs.

HOW DO YOU KNOW WHEN YOU ARE IN SERIOUS FINANCIAL TROUBLE?

There are a number of signs that show you have debt problems. These signs include:

- You do not have enough money to pay your debts and live.
- More than 20 percent of what you earn is used to repay interest on debt.
- You find you are running up more debt to live.
- Institutions become less keen to lend you money.
- You find you have to pay higher interest rates than before because you are now considered a credit risk. This means that lenders fear that you will be unable to repay your debt.
- You are having sleepless nights worrying about what to do.

WHAT TO DO IF YOU ARE IN SERIOUS FINANCIAL TROUBLE

- If you have investments, cash them in and pay off the debt. If your investments are in assurance policies and there is a penalty for cashing them in, take a loan against the policy and use the money to reduce debt.
- If you are making monthly investments, stop the investments and use the money to pay off debt. The only exception here is contributions to a life assurance policy or a retirement fund. If you are in a really bad way, you can ask the life assurance company to make your policy paid up. You leave the money you have invested where it is, but stop paying the premiums.
- Do not borrow any more money.
- Cut up any credit cards you have.
- Cut back on your standard of living any way you can, particularly spending on luxuries. Even going to the movies is a luxury. If you do not budget, you need to start budgeting now, to ensure you are controlling your spending.
- Go and see your creditors (the people to whom you owe money). Explain your predicament and what you are trying to do to solve your problem. Your creditors will not want to take you to court as that costs money. If

they see you are trying to do something to solve the problem they will be more sympathetic.
- Pay off high-interest debt first.
- Avoid dealing with people who advertise in newspapers that they can solve your debt problems. In most cases these people are what are called loan sharks, who will take over all or part of your debt and charge you a much higher interest rate.

YOUR CREDIT RATING

Your credit rating is something banks and other institutions give you when you want to borrow money or open an account. A good credit rating results in it being easier for you to borrow money and, most importantly, get lower interest rates when you do borrow. A good credit rating is a very precious thing to keep throughout your life. A number of factors are taken into account when you are given a credit rating. These include:
- **Education:** The higher your level of education and your potential earning power, the better.
- **Type of job:** The better paid the job and the better your chances of promotion, the more creditors will like you.
- **Job history:** If you have been in one job for a long time. It does not matter what the job is – even working at the same restaurant since you were 15 will count. It shows you are a stable person to be trusted.
- **Your bank account:** Get your bank to appreciate having you as a customer by not doing things like bouncing cheques (issuing cheques when there is no money in your account). If a bank sees that even as a teenager you were saving money on a regular basis, the manager will be impressed and will mark you up on the creditworthiness scale.
- **Past credit history:** You have always repaid any loans or accounts you have had on time. If you have defaulted on a loan or an account in the past, your name is likely to be reported to credit assessment companies, who then keep your name on a list to warn others that they should not lend you money, or they should charge you very high interest rates.

Isn't it amazing? The people who insist that you have a good credit rating are the very ones who are trying to wreck it by lending you as much money as possible. Makes you think!

DIFFERENT FORMS OF DEBT

Debt comes in many different forms, but the main distinguishing factor is the interest rate that is charged. There is a law called the Usury Act, which limits the amount of interest you can be charged. However, on small amounts of money under R10 000 you can be charged any amount of interest, and loan sharks do just that. Some people are paying interest rates of more than 1 000 percent a year to loan sharks.

When borrowing, you need to understand the different types of interest rates.

PRIME OVERDRAFT LENDING RATE

Most interest rates are based on what is called the prime overdraft lending rate. This is the interest rate at which banks lend money to their very best customers, mostly big companies. Many interest rates are described as being over the prime rate or less than the prime rate. An average bank customer can expect to pay between 2 and 3 percent above the prime rate for an overdraft, but below the prime rate for home loans because the banks have the security of being able to repossess your home if you do not pay up.

You get two primary forms of interest-lending rates (interest rates at which you borrow money). These are:

- **Variable rates:** These are interest rates that go up or down depending on what is happening in the wider economy. Most interest-lending rates, including the prime rate, are variable rates of interest. As many interest rates are linked to the prime rate, they will go up or down in line with the prime rate. These are called prime-linked variable interest rates; and
- **Fixed rates:** These are interest rates you agree to when you borrow money. The rate cannot be increased or decreased over the period of the loan. Very few loans have fixed rates. Most fixed rates apply when you invest money.

Interest rates go up or down for a number of reasons. These include:

- **High inflation:** If inflation is high, investors will only lend money to banks or anyone else wanting to borrow money if they can get a real rate of return. A real rate of return on an investment is an interest rate that is more than the inflation rate. (For example, if the return you are receiving is 10 percent a year, but the inflation rate is 7 percent a year, you are receiving a real rate of return of 3 percent a year.)

- **Foreign investor confidence:** This is a major factor in South Africa, where we do not have enough money saved by ourselves to meet all the borrowing requirements, especially of the government and big companies. The only way we can get foreign investors to lend us money is by offering high interest rates. If we offer them high interest rates, the same interest rates must be paid to local investors and savers. The result is everyone, including the government, must pay high interest rates for the money that is borrowed.

Here are examples of different types of debt and the type of interest you can expect to pay:

- **Family and friends:** This is generally the cheapest form of debt, usually considerably below the prime rate. The usual arrangement is to split the difference between bank lending and borrowing rates. If you take the interest rate that you pay a bank if you borrow money, and the interest rate the friend or relative would receive if they invest the money with the bank, you total the two rates and divide by two. For example, if you could borrow money at 15 percent and your mother could get 10 percent for saving her money, you would pay her 12.5 percent a year in interest. A word of warning: you must ensure that you repay the debt on schedule. If you take advantage of a relative or friend by not repaying the debt, it can make for uncool vibes.
- **Education loans:** Most education loans are made by banks at very favourable terms, because they hope to have you as a well-educated, creditworthy and loyal customer when you have graduated. These loans are normally up to 3 percent below the prime rate and will be variable, linked to the prime rate. (See Chapter 6.)
- **Home loans** (also known as housing mortgage bonds): Interest on housing mortgage bonds is normally the lowest rate for an individual. Most home loan rates are variable (they can be changed by the bank with one month's notice, normally in line with changes in the prime rate), and can be up to 3 percent lower than any other interest rate you will pay.
- **Overdrafts** (loans on your current account at your bank): The rate is variable and based on the prime rate. Depending on your credit record you could pay, in worst cases, more than 10 percent over prime, but in good cases, 3 or 4 percent over prime.

- **Loans against assurance policies:** Interest on these loans is normally quite low, but because you have borrowed the money against your investment, your investment is now lower and it is earning lower returns. The result is that the total cost of the loan is greater than it appears. Normally you will only be able to borrow about 80 percent of the investment amount you have accumulated.
- **Hire purchase:** This method of borrowing is used mainly in the furniture industry and when you borrow to buy a car. The rates are very high, often close to the maximum permitted under the Usury Act. Effectively you are hiring or leasing the car until you have paid off the debt. There are often additional charges, particularly if you pay off the debt sooner.
- **Leasing agreements:** These agreements are normally used by the motor vehicle industry. They are similar to hire purchase agreements, but you do not necessarily take ownership at the end of the rental period. Interest rates are similar to hire purchase rates.
- **Credit cards:** This is some of the easiest credit you can get, but be warned: it is very expensive, with rates being close to the Usury Act maximum. If you are an impulse buyer you should not have a credit card. Credit cards are a very easy way to get into financial trouble.
- **Informal sector borrowing:** If you need to borrow from this sector, which includes loan sharks, then you are in serious trouble, as you do not have an acceptable credit record. You will be robbed.

HOW TO GET LOWER INTEREST RATES

There are ways to pay lower interest rates. Here are a few tips:

- **Negotiate:** Never accept the first rate you are offered.
- **Be mercenary:** Don't be a loyal customer. See if you can get a better rate from a competitive bank.
- **Credit rating:** Make sure you always have a good credit rating. Always pay any debt you have on time. This will ensure a lower rate.
- **Your bank account:** Always run your bank accounts responsibly and never issue dud cheques.
- **Employers:** Sometimes employers arrange that their employees get lower rates.
- **Watch for surprises:** Read all contracts carefully. There may be hidden penalties for late payments or even for paying back a loan early.

6

Education

Education is the single major issue in your future financial success. It is worth investing both time and money in your education. It will never be wasted. A good education is essential for your future well-being. It does not matter which career path you choose. Whether you want to be a plumber, a game ranger, a lawyer, an accountant, a blacksmith or a financial adviser, it is essential you get the best qualifications available for the job. Education will not be the only key to a successful career, nor will it guarantee you a job, or that you will own and manage a successful business, but it will play a major part.

Your options for generating an income for the rest of your life depend largely upon your education, talents and skills. Getting the education and training needed for a better job could be the best investment you make. However, you must ask yourself whether the education is appropriate and whether it will provide what you really want from life.

You need to consider a number of issues when deciding on a tertiary (post-matric) education. It is not merely an issue of what interests you now.

Issues you need to take into account include:

- Your skills and interests.
- The long-term income expectations for your chosen career field.
- The future prospects for your chosen career field. For example, recently in South Africa the clothing industry took a tremendous knock because manufacturers found cheaper and better skilled workers in other countries. Consider what your skills would be worth in a truly open, worldwide market.
- The durability of your skills into the future. Knowledge is the key to survival in the years ahead, whether you're a carpenter or a computer programmer, but the pace of innovation is staggering. There are many mainframe computer specialists who lost their jobs in the eighties because they failed to see the move to computer networks. Nothing has a more disastrous impact on financial security than a lengthy period of unemployment.
- Whether you will be happy in the job. It is no good wanting to be in the medical field simply because of the status and earnings when you cannot stand the sight of blood.

THE COST OF EDUCATION

Many families struggle to pay off the car, buy enough food, pay for their home and pay their kids' high-school costs. They are simply unable to save to pay for further education demands after the kids leave school.

The struggle to pay for tertiary education is not unique to South Africa. In one of the world's richest countries, the United States of America, it is also a major issue. Most teenagers are actually expected to make a large contribution towards paying for their own education. And if you think education is expensive here, in Japan, where education is considered one of the most important things in life, an average of 25 percent of the family budget goes towards education.

Education can be divided into three periods: the school period, the tertiary period and continual learning for the rest of your life.

Many financial advisers say that parents should pay for their children's school education from their monthly income while saving for their tertiary education. In the United States, many financial advisers say parents should not invest in the tertiary education of their children if it is going to undermine their own long-term savings plans, such as having sufficient money for retirement. Parents should rather look after themselves and let their children invest in their own future.

Good education is becoming increasingly expensive in South Africa. One year at university in 2002 could have cost about R15 000 in tuition fees alone. This does not include all the extra costs such as textbooks, research materials, transport and accommodation (particularly if your home is in another town). If your parents started saving when you were one year old to meet education costs of R40 000 when you turned 19 in 2002, they would have had to save R185 a month. This would have seemed a reasonable target at the time, but the increasing costs of education were unlikely to be foreseen. Total costs a year, including fees, books, clothing, food and accommodation, are likely to be more than R50 000 a year in 2003.

For many parents the cost of education after you have finished school is impossibly expensive. If you were lucky, your parents would have taken out an education investment when you were young, and they may now have part or all the money required to educate you. But then you are among the lucky few.

There are a number of different types of savings vehicles dedicated to education savings. These include:

- **Life assurance investments:** Education investment and life policies that can be bought through life assurance companies. Education policies not only provide a savings vehicle, but your parents can also take out life assurance that will result in your university fees being fully or partially paid if they die or are no longer able to work because of illness or disability.

- **Unit trust funds:** Here your parents should still take out assurance to ensure that if they die or are unable to work your education costs will be met.

FINANCING YOUR EDUCATION

You have a number of options in financing your tertiary education. One way or another you should be able to find the money to pay to be a student at varsity or tech. Here are the main options. Most of the options work in combination with each other. You should use every source of finance available to you.

YOURSELF

If you know your parents are struggling financially, you should start taking responsibility for yourself in your school years. Get a job or start a small business, and save part of the money you make towards your education. You will need to continue working when you are studying. Many students fund their entire education programme themselves by taking a part-time job. You could suggest to people who give you presents, such as your grandparents, that they should rather contribute to your education savings.

BURSARIES AND SCHOLARSHIPS

Bursaries and scholarships can be hard to come by in South Africa, particularly if you are a white student. Because many blacks were given an inferior education in the years of apartheid and mainly come from very poor homes, quite rightly most bursaries and scholarships currently go to people who come from deprived backgrounds. There are a wide range of bursaries and scholarships available. You should check with the educational institution where you will study to find out what is available. The institutions all have lists, and you will be amazed at what bursaries are available and under what conditions. Some are given if you excel in sport, others are given by religious organisations and some are very narrowly defined. For example, you may find that there are bursaries for any member of the Idukat family. So, if your family name were Idukat, you would have a very good chance of qualifying. There will not be many other Idukats!

A number of factors determine how bursaries, and particularly scholarships, are granted. The most important of these are: needs; family assets, including all savings and investments; number of students in the family drawing on family assets as well as other expenses; family income; the study course you are taking; and your ability as a student (straight As, or at least a few, in your matric results will always help).

In the past, many companies have also given loans or bursaries to hard-working students who do well. There is no harm in writing letters to every company you know that would employ someone with the type of qualifications you are seeking. You may get lucky. All it will cost you is your time writing letters, compiling your curriculum vitae, photocopying all your qualifications and references, and the cost of the stamps to mail all the documents. Increasingly, companies that do provide bursaries only do so after the first year when you have proved yourself.

LOANS

When all else fails you will have to resort to borrowing money. Borrowing to pay for an education is a good investment. You are investing in yourself to make yourself a sellable commodity.

You must remember that borrowing money to pay for education is still debt. You will have to repay the money, and this can be very arduous. When you start earning an income you will have many demands made on your money. Repaying the debt will mean that you will have to go short in many other areas. It is going to be a case of 'young, educated, but broke' for a few years.

It is important for your future financial well-being that you keep borrowing to a minimum by doing part-time and vacation work to supplement your expenses. Fortunately the tourism industry is growing rapidly in South Africa, and this is increasingly providing for seasonal work that is timed with the summer holidays.

BORROWING SOURCES

There are a number of different ways to borrow money. These are the main sources of education loans:

- **Your parents' employers:** Many employers will give interest-free or low-interest loans to their employees to help pay for the education of their children. The main problem with these loans is that they normally have to be repaid within 12 months. However, most employers will negotiate the circumstances of the repayment.
- **A future employer:** If you are fortunate enough to have found someone who is prepared to employ you when you are qualified, they will often

assist you with a loan. If you are extremely lucky, the repayment terms are: firstly, that you must keep passing your examinations; and secondly, that as long as you work for the company for a predetermined number of years after qualifying, you do not have to repay the loan. These arrangements are normally only made when you have proved yourself by passing your first year successfully.

The most common area where this type of arrangement is made is where you are undergoing an apprenticeship to qualify as an artisan in a trade; or you are involved in an area where there is a shortage of skills, such as a chartered accountant. If you are successful in making such an arrangement, you are normally expected to work for the company part time and/or during vacations. Another bonus is that you nearly always get paid for the part-time work.

- **The Tertiary Education Fund:** This is a public company established to receive donations, which are made available to deserving and financially needy students. You are issued with a loan, part of which is converted to a bursary at the end of each academic year, depending on your results. Repayment of the loan only starts when your income reaches a certain level after you start working. You can get details of the fund and how to apply from the educational institution you plan to attend.
- **Your parents' home loan:** Home loans can have preferential rates of up to 3 percent below the prime lending rate at which banks lend money to their better customers. You must compare the interest rate with what you would pay a bank for an educational loan.
- **Banks:** In recent years banks have started making very preferential, low-interest loans to students. Not only are you offered preferential loans, but you can also take advantage of other services offered by the banks at preferential rates.

The conditions and other add-on services differ from bank to bank, so you need to make a checklist and see what is best for you. What follows is a compilation of information received from a number of banks.

QUALIFICATIONS FOR A BANK LOAN

Students who are registered at a university or technikon, and who are studying either part time or full time, can qualify for a bank education loan. A student can apply for a loan at any stage from the start of year one. You can also apply if you are registered at some other type of educational institution, but the banks may be a bit reticent to provide a loan if they do not see much prospect of you finding a job with the education you are trying to get. If you are studying for a University of South Africa (Unisa) degree either directly or through a private college, you will also qualify for a bank loan. Banks often require one of your parents to be a customer when you apply for a loan.

The amount you can borrow

The amount a bank may be prepared to lend you will depend on the course you are doing, but it should be more than enough to cover tuition fees and books, and even part or all of your residence fees, if you are not living at home. One bank will even lend you pocket money.

Interest rates

The interest rate varies depending on the course you are doing. If you are doing a course that will lead you to earn a top salary, you are likely to pay less. This may seem strange, but the reason for this is that banks want top-earning customers and people who will head companies, making banking decisions. All interest rates are favourable and are below the prime rate at which banks lend to their best customers. Postgraduate students often get interest rates that are half the prime rate!

Loan repayment periods

The amount of time you are given to repay an education loan varies from bank to bank. Normally, if you are a full-time student, you have to pay the interest as it falls due (monthly), but you do not have to start paying the capital amount of the loan until you have completed your studies. It is, however, preferable to start repaying the capital amount as soon as possible, as it gets bigger every year and you will have to pay more interest.

The capital must normally be repaid over the same period it took you to get your qualification. So, if you did a three-year course, you are likely to be expected to repay the capital within three years of starting work. If you have to undergo an apprenticeship or articles, you can negotiate with the bank to extend the repayment period until you are qualified and earning a proper salary.

If you are a part-time student, you may be required to start repaying both the capital and interest from when you receive the loan.

Security

Your parents or legal guardian will have to agree to repay the loan if you default. You will also be required to take out life assurance to cover the amount of the loan in case you die or become disabled.

What happens if you fail or drop out?

If you fail your examinations in any year, the bank may not give you a loan for your repeat year. If you drop out you will have to repay the loan under the same conditions that apply if you pass. For example, if you drop out after two years, you will have two years to repay the loan and any interest.

Other benefits

You normally qualify for a special bank account on which you do not need to keep a minimum balance, on which there are no charges and on which interest is paid on your credit balance. You may also qualify for other benefits, such as preferential interest rate car loans, a credit card and/or cheque account (to be avoided if possible).

Renewing your loan each year

For every year that you want to maintain and continue your loan, you will have to send your bank manager proof that you have passed the previous year's exams, and that you have registered as a student for the current year.

Whichever way you choose to finance your education, you should plan early to get the best package to suit your needs.

7

Getting
a Job

Jobs are a rare commodity in South Africa. Getting one, unless you are very lucky, extremely talented or marry the boss's daughter, will be a job in itself. But you can move the odds quite considerably in your favour if you go about it in the correct way. This chapter is divided into three parts. Part one is about how to get a job; part two on how to keep it; and part three is about your rights and employment benefits as an employee.

FINDING A JOB

Obviously the more skills and experience you have, the easier it becomes to find a job. This is where education is so important. The better educated you are, the easier it will be to find the job you are seeking. This does not mean that you should indiscriminately get any qualification. The more qualifications you can get that are associated with the job you want, the better it will be for you. Assuming that you already have the qualifications for the job that you are attempting to find, you must follow a number of fairly simple steps in applying for the job you want.

1. PREPARE A CURRICULUM VITAE OR CV

Your curriculum vitae, or history of your life, is the first impression you make on your potential employer, so make it good.

Ground rules for a good first impression

You must ensure that your curriculum vitae (also called a résumé):

- Contains all the important issues about you.
- Is typed and neatly laid out (use a professional typist if necessary).
- Contains no grammatical or spelling mistakes.
- Is absolutely accurate and truthful.

You do not need to spell out every detail of your life, such as when you lost your milk teeth. But you should consider what important facts your new employer is likely to want to know and provide backup evidence such as university degrees, technikon diplomas, matriculation certificates or any other qualification, as well as references from employers for whom you have worked, even in a casual position.

The basic structure of your curriculum vitae should be:

NAME

ADDRESS

CONTACT TELEPHONE NUMBER

IDENTIFICATION NUMBER

DATE OF BIRTH

PLACE OF BIRTH

CONDITION OF HEALTH (If you have a problem, explain the details)

CITIZENSHIP

MARITAL STATUS

DEPENDANTS (If any)

MOTOR VEHICLE LICENCE DETAILS

TAX NUMBER (If you have one)

CURRENT EMPLOYMENT

EDUCATION (Start from the highest qualification down to the lowest)

WORK EXPERIENCE (Start with your latest job and work backwards. Give dates, a description of the job and the name and address of the employer. If you have written or verbal references, give details.)

GENERAL (Any other experience, such as working for community organisations. This can be very important, as it is an indication of what type of person you are.)

SPECIAL ACHIEVEMENTS (This includes such things as sporting achievements, being a school prefect and serving on a student representative council.)

INTERESTS, HOBBIES AND SPORTS (These should be genuine. For example, if you put down birdwatching because you have heard that is the interest of one of your bosses, you could be caught out if he or she sits in at an interview and asks you about the mating call of the black eagle.)

Stick to what is relevant: An employer does not want to know about such things as boy or girlfriends, or whether you are a vegetarian, or whistle catchy little tunes.

See pages 74–75 for an example of a curriculum vitae.

2. WHERE TO FIND A JOB

Once you know what you want to do, the next challenge is to identify potential employers. There are a number of ways you can do this. It will need a bit of research on your part.

- **Newspaper advertisements:** Newspapers and financial magazines always have numerous jobs advertised. A number of newspapers also publish job-finder supplements.
- **Trade magazines:** If you are seeking to get into a particular trade or profession, you will often find that there are specialist magazines for that profession. These magazines will not only give you an idea of job availability, but also names of companies. You can get details of these magazines from career counsellors or people in a similar job.
- **Employment agencies:** There are quite a large number of employment agencies, which seek staff on behalf of companies. You will find their names in newspaper advertisements. You will need to register with an employment agency.

Example of a curriculum vitae

Name:	Jill Smith
Address:	23 Oak Avenue, Newtown, 96768
Telephone Number:	(076) 66 6868
ID Number:	140379509007
Date of Birth:	14 March 1979
Place of Birth:	Melmoth, KwaZulu-Natal
Condition of Health:	Excellent
Citizenship:	South African
Marital Status:	Unmarried
Dependants:	Nil
Driver's Licence:	Motor car licence (obtained in 1999)
Tax Number:	786092713A
Current Employment:	Working as a part-time waitress at the Butcher Shop, Sandton

Educational Qualifications

Highest Education Qualification:	BSc (Hons) University of the Witwatersrand
Additional Post-Matric Qualification:	Diploma in Computer Proficiency, Damelin College

Educational Institutions Attended

2002:	Postgraduate at the University of the Witwatersrand (Diploma and results attached)
January 1999 to December 2001:	Undergraduate at the University of the Witwatersrand. Majors: Physics and Chemistry (Diploma and results attached)

- **Professional organisations:** Many professions have professional organisations. They will often have lists of employers and even job vacancies.
- **Employee organisations (trade unions):** Trade unions will often be able to help, particularly if you are a member.
- **Employer organisations:** There are many such organisations. Some of them are broad-based, like your local Chamber of Commerce; or narrow-based, like the Chamber of Mines. They will have lists of potential employers in your field.

January to July 1998:	Damelin College Computer School (Diploma attached)
1993 to 1997:	Eshowe High School (Matriculation certificate attached)
1986 to 1992:	Melmoth Junior School

Work Experience:

December vacations from 1999 and current:	Part-time waitress at the Butcher Shop, Sandton Square. Written reference attached.
July to December 1998:	Worked for three months at Charly's Computers, Piccadilly Circus in London. Written reference attached.
1997 (Matric year):	Shadow experience at Addition and Subtraction Accountants, Eshowe. Written reference attached.

General:

Member of the Young Lions, Hyde Park branch

Special Achievements:

Eshowe High School: First-team netball
University of the Witwatersrand: U21 netball team

Interests, Sports and Hobbies:

Music
Skateboarding
Netball
Reading

- **Community notice boards:** These advertisements, which you will find in places such as public libraries and supermarkets, will tend to advertise jobs of a more casual nature.

3. APPROACHING POTENTIAL EMPLOYERS

There are two basic approaches to potential employers: replying to an advertisement; or, more difficult, cold-calling. Both involve writing a letter of application.

Basic rules for a job application letter

- Be brief: Keep you letter to the point. Do not write more than one page.
- Be neat: Type the letter, unless you are specifically asked that it be handwritten.
- Be accurate: Check and recheck your letter for grammatical and spelling errors.
- Be specific: Do not make a general enquiry about whether the company has 'any jobs'. Say what kind of job you are seeking and why.
- Names: Attempt to find out the name of the person to whom you are writing (for instance, by telephoning the company and finding out the name of the human resources manager). Make absolutely sure that you have spelt the name correctly. People like to be addressed by their name, particularly when it is correctly spelt.
- Backing documentation: Attach backup documentation such as curriculum vitae, references and diplomas. (Only use copies, not the originals, of precious diplomas.) At the foot of your letter, type a list of the attached documents.
- Contact address and telephone numbers: This is essential for a reply.
- Do not send assembly line letters: This means not photocopying one letter and merely adding a handwritten address at the top.
- Copies: Keep a copy of every letter you have sent so that you know what you have said and not said. This is important for if and when you get an interview.

Your letter of application is your **prospective** employer's **first impression** of you. Make it **good**.

Basic rules for replying to an advertisement

The advertisement will give you details of how you should respond. If you are required to write an application letter, keep it brief and to the point. Again, ensure that it is neatly typed and contains no grammatical or spelling errors.

Do not write rambling or gushy letters. Be brief and professional. The reader wants the facts in a quickly digestible form – not an explanation of how the world should work.

Example of a letter responding to an advertisement

23 Oak Avenue
Newtown
96768
3 December 2002

Ms VI Person

The Human Resources Director
Marigold Technologies
597 West Street
Sandton

Dear Ms Person

Employment vacancy: Laboratory technician

I am replying to your advertisement in the *Saturday Star* of 2 December. I would like to apply for the above position.

I have recently graduated from the University of the Witwatersrand with a BSc (Hons) majoring in chemistry and physics. My intention in studying this course was to become a laboratory technician working for a research company such as yours.

I am currently working as a part-time waitress, but I am available at short notice for an interview. I can be contacted at telephone number 011 66 6868.

I enclose my curriculum vitae, copies of pertinent references, certificates and details of my qualifications in support of my application.

I look forward to hearing from you.

Yours sincerely,

Jill Smith

Cold-calling

From your earlier research you will have a list of potential employers. Write to the human resources manager of the company, or the managing director if the company does not have a human resources department, telling them who you are and why you would like to work for the company. Try to find out something about the company before you write, so that you can put in just one line showing that you have a definite interest in what they do.

Do not walk into any businesses and ask for a job without making a prior appointment either in writing or by telephone. The person will probably be busy, get irritated and will just say: No.

Example of a cold-call letter

23 Oak Avenue
Newtown
96768
3 December 2002

Ms VI Person

The Human Resources Director
Marigold Technologies
597 West Street
Sandton

Dear Ms Person

Employment Application

I have recently graduated from the University of the Witwatersrand with a BSc (Hons) majoring in chemistry and physics. My intention in studying this course was to become a laboratory technician working for a research company such as yours.

While at university I came across the name of your company when research on toothpaste development was discussed. I believe I am suitably qualified to make a contribution to the work being done by Marigold Technologies. Currently I am working as a part-time waitress, but I am available at short notice for an interview. I can be contacted at telephone number 66 6868.

I enclose my curriculum vitae, copies of pertinent references, certificates and details of my qualifications in support of my application.

I look forward to hearing from you.

Yours sincerely,

Jill Smith

4. JOB APPLICATION FORM

Most employers require you to complete a job application form after your initial application. Before filling in any answers, read the form from beginning to end and make sure you understand the questions. Ask for help if you require it, but don't ask questions merely for the sake of doing so. Make sure you fill in the form precisely and do not make spelling errors. Photocopy the form to do a trial run, or attempt to get a spare form so that the final document is clean.

5. THE APPOINTMENT

Once you have an appointment you are quite a bit of the way there, but remember other people are probably after the job as well, so here are a few hints to give you an edge:

- Be normal: Do not try to look extraordinary. For example, take the ring out of your eyebrow.
- Be smart: Dress in clean, smart clothes.
- Don't go over the top: Be conservative with make-up and perfumes.
- Be punctual: Arrive at the business premises early and wait outside until a few minutes before your appointment so that you report for the interview precisely on time. (If there is a security procedure, allow time for this as well.)
- Do not gush: Job interviews make everyone nervous and we can all tend to talk too much. Try to answer questions clearly, briefly and precisely. However, do not go to the other extreme and grunt 'yes' or 'no' or 'dunno'.
- Look people in the eye: Don't spend the interview looking under the table.
- Speak up: Do not mumble your answers. If necessary, take a few seconds of silence to think out a proper reply.
- Don't criticise former employers: Employers stick together. They will be concerned about what you may say about them in the future.
- Your portfolio: Have a copy of all your correspondence with the prospective employer, any other relevant documentation and any examples you may have of your work in a tidy folder.
- Get details: Find out about the business before you arrive so that the person interviewing you can see that you have an interest in the business. At a bare minimum, have the name of the managing director. If the company is listed on the Johannesburg Stock Exchange, get a copy of the annual report. Telephone the receptionist at the company after you

are granted an interview; explain who you are and ask if there are any reports or descriptions of the company and how you can get copies.

- Be prepared: Try to think of the type of questions you may be asked and replies to the questions. The person interviewing you will also probably ask you if you have any questions. Think out any questions you may have beforehand, such as the hours you will work, transport (if you need it), whether the company has a code of conduct and/or a mission statement, and what additional training you can get. Do not ask about pay upfront. Rather let the interviewer raise the issue, but have an idea of what you want when asked. If the issue is not raised, ask if you can be given a general idea about the full remuneration package that may go with the position, including pension, medical aid and leave.

- Do not ask frivolous questions: Keep your questions about the job to the point. Don't ask the interviewer how many children he or she has or ask about their suntan.

- Establish the next step: If you are not told at the end of the interview what the next step will be, you should ask how you will be informed on whether you will be employed or not.

- Follow-up issues: Have a pen and small notebook with you at the interview to note down such things as the date and time of any follow-up interview; further information the employer may want from you; and important information you are given, such as details of the proposed employment package.

- Say thank you: good manners always help.

6. WHEN YOU ARE GIVEN THE JOB

When you have been given the job, write a letter saying thank you. You will also probably be given some type of letter of appointment or contract. This letter of appointment will contain the essential details of your job, such as what will be required of you and what you will receive in return. Read this document very carefully. Query anything that does not correspond with what you were told. Keep the document in a safe place; it could be important in the future, if there is ever a dispute between you and your employer. If you are not required to sign a contract or a letter of appointment, it is probably wise for you to write a letter to your new employer recording how you understand the terms of your employment.

1. PREPARE A CURRICULUM VITAE OR CV

2. WHERE TO FIND A JOB

3. APPROACHING POTENTIAL EMPLOYERS

4. JOB APPLICATION FORM

5. THE APPOINTMENT

6. WHEN YOU ARE GIVEN THE JOB

KEEPING YOUR JOB

Getting the job is only part of the challenge. You need to keep the job and do it well enough so that your pay is increased and you can get promotion. Here are some tips on how to be seen as a valuable employee:

- Be punctual: Always arrive on time and never leave early unless your employer suggests it.
- Be thorough: Never do a sloppy job or leave the job incomplete. If you cannot finish on time, return as soon as possible to complete the job.
- Be obliging: Never say, 'That's not my job.'
- Be honest: Nothing will undermine you more quickly than being dishonest. One lie will be enough for people to treat you with suspicion for a very long time.
- Be trustworthy: If you are entrusted with confidential information, keep it confidential. Don't tell other employees, and particularly not outsiders, in an attempt to appear important. For many firms the business edge they have is a special way of doing something. If this information becomes common knowledge because you cannot keep quiet, you could well be undermining your own job.
- Accept responsibility: If something goes wrong and it is your fault, accept the blame. Do not attempt to blame others, particularly not someone who is your junior.
- Be friendly: Everyone cheers up in response to a friendly greeting and a smile. Try to use a person's name when you speak to them. Don't bring your problems from home to work. Because you had a rough night on the town with little sleep is no reason to get annoyed with your colleagues.
- Be professional: This includes presenting your work neatly and efficiently; not being continually flippant if you are involved in a discussion (the occasional joke is fine, but don't try to be the court jester); and not fudging issues when you do not know the answer (say that you do not know, and make sure you find out the answer as quickly as possible).
- Dress appropriately: Although dress in the workplace is becoming increasingly casual, do try to dress as your employer would expect, particularly if you come into contact with the public. Establish if there is a company dress code. Always wear clean and neat clothes. If you don't take yourself seriously, no one else will.

- Improve your knowledge: Whenever you get the opportunity to improve your knowledge of the job you are doing or of the company, take it. This will make you a more valuable employee.
- Don't be overfamiliar: Don't treat your seniors as casual pals. Speak to them with respect.

DEALING WITH CUSTOMERS

Most jobs, particularly in the fast-growing services sector, entail working with customers. If your job includes dealing with the public or customers in any way, it is essential that you accept that you have a very important role. Remember at all times that it is the customer who is paying your salary – not your employer. Every interaction a customer has with you is the impression the customer gets of the company, rather than of you as a person. If you keep clashing with customers, no matter how right you may be, you are not likely to keep your job for long.

Some hints for dealing with customers

- Be knowledgeable: Find out from colleagues about the type of questions customers may ask and establish the answers.
- The customer is always right: Accept that the customer is always right, even though they may be wrong. Even when they are clearly wrong, attempt to resolve a situation without embarrassing the customer. Never make accusatory remarks. Rather refer to 'misunderstandings'.
- Don't keep customers waiting: There is nothing more irritating than people who are supposed to be supplying a service standing around chatting to each other, ignoring customers.
- Be professional: If you cannot deal with a problem or query, find someone who can.
- Always follow up: If you have delegated a customer problem to someone else, check back to ensure that the problem has been resolved. If possible, telephone the customer and ensure they are satisfied.
- Meet commitments: If you have given a commitment, say to return a telephone call, then make sure you do it.
- Creating an impression: There is nothing that impresses an employer more than flattering comments from a customer about one of the staff, and there is nothing that upsets an employer more than a lost customer.

YOUR JOB AND THE LAW

With the tightening-up of legislation and far greater protection for employees, the detailing of your conditions of employment has become a vital aspect of a job. There are three main issues that control your conditions of employment. These are:

- **Labour law:** There are various laws, of which the Labour Relations Act and the Basic Conditions of Employment Act are the most important. The various laws lay down the basic conditions of your employment, including your rights and obligations and your employer's rights and obligations.
- **Trade union, staff association and professional association agreements:** Even if you are not a member of a trade union or association you can still be affected by an agreement. You need to find out about these from your human resources department or from a member of the union or association. If you are a member you still need to find out about any agreements. These agreements often govern pay and other working conditions.
- **Your employment contract:** You should always ensure that you receive an employment contract, which is signed by both your employer and yourself. The contract should set down the parameters of your employment, including your pay package (current and future), a description of your job, your hours of work and any other special arrangements. You must read this contract carefully and question anything about which you feel unsure or insecure. The contract has to be within the parameters of the law, and any union or professional agreements.

YOUR PACKAGE

There is an almost endless list of items that may be included in your total employment package. Not all of them will necessarily be listed in your employment contract, as many are at the discretion of your employer and will be dependent on many factors, including the size of the company, your usefulness to your employer and the amount of profit your company makes.

Your employment contract should detail the basics such as pay, working hours, leave, retirement and medical benefits. The extent of your package and contract will depend on your seniority, the responsibility of your job, your authority over others, experience, your qualifications and skills, and your potential value to the company. In previous years issues such as age or gender were also taken into consideration. However, to discriminate against anyone on any grounds such as gender, age or disability is now illegal. There is still some legal discrimination on the grounds of race, with affirmative employment practices that help previously disadvantaged groups in the workplace.

Employment contracts are no longer limited to people in full-time employment. If you are a casual, part-time or contract employee, you should also be given a contract detailing the terms of your employment.

There is an almost endless list of items that may be included in your package. In alphabetical order, these include:

Allowances: There are many different items that fall under this category, of which the best known are car (known as travelling allowances) and entertainment allowances. There are also a number of job-specific allowances that are often paid. For example, if you are an artisan you may receive a tool allowance; danger pay if you are a miner; a clothing allowance if you are a receptionist at a very public-oriented company; or a telephone allowance if you have to be in constant contact with the office or customers.

Bonuses: Bonuses can come in a number of different forms and are nearly always at the discretion of your employer. Bonuses are often linked to the profits made by the company. Bonuses include:

- Annual bonus: Many employers pay their employees a 'double cheque' or 'thirteenth cheque' once a year. A double cheque, however, does not always mean exactly that. It can be more or less than your annual salary. A bonus is usually paid at the discretion of the employer; or it may be a fixed amount or percentage of your pay written into your contract. Most employers pay an annual bonus in December; others pay it at the end of their financial year when they know how good or bad profits have been; or others, such as the civil service, pay up in the month of your birthday.
- Profit-share bonus: Some employers pay profit-share bonuses. These bonuses are still rare and are normally paid as a 'fourteenth cheque'. They may only be paid on an individual basis, while other employers will give a profit incentive bonus to an entire department, which is then split

up according to seniority. The key to the bonus is that profits above a certain level must be made.

- Long-term service bonus (loyalty): These bonuses are paid in various ways. Some companies may give you a special award after you have been employed for a certain number of years. For example, long service bonuses may be paid after 10, 20 and 30 years. Or you may get a special bonus every year based on the number of years you have been employed.

Car or travelling allowances: These allowances come in a number of different forms. You may get a company car; receive payment for every kilometre driven in your own car (this is normally based on mileage rates drawn up by the Automobile Association); or a monthly allowance to purchase a car. Travelling allowances are normally only given to senior members of staff. However, if you need to use a car to do your job (for example, you are in sales), you may also receive a travelling allowance. If you use your own car, you should at least ensure that you are recompensed at the AA rate.

Company housing: This is a disappearing perk. Some years ago, many senior management staff were given company homes where they stayed for free or paid a low rental. The main reason for this perk disappearing is that it is now taxed as income. However, housing is often still provided, without a tax penalty, where people are in jobs that require them to be in different areas for comparatively short periods of time. Examples are relief staff who are sent around the country, and construction workers for companies that get contracts all around the country, if not the world.

Discount prices: You may be allowed to buy goods produced or sold by your employer at discount prices. Your employer may also have agreements with other companies to provide discounts to staff. I know of breweries in Europe that give their staff free beer, although I don't think they can drink on duty! Incidentally, a system that was used fairly commonly by wine farmers, known as the *dop* system, in which workers were given liquor instead of all their pay, is now illegal.

Education and training assistance: Many employers will pay for you to receive extra training and education (see Further Training below), and often also provide you with assistance in educating your children with low or interest-free loans.

Entertainment allowance: Again, entertainment allowances are normally only given to senior members of staff or staff who are involved in interacting with customers, such as sales staff. Entertainment allowances can be paid in a number of ways. You may be given a fixed amount a month, or you may be reimbursed for your actual expenditure.

Grading: Many larger companies have grading structures, which describe the job rather than the person holding it. The grading of the job depends on a number of factors, including the level of skill or education required, the level of authority, responsibility for other workers and level of decision-making. The level of your grading will often define many aspects of your package. As you go up the grading scales, so your package will expand and increase. Each grading band normally comes with an upper, average and lower level of pay. It is useful to find out about how any grading system works. This will give you an idea of what you will need to progress up the ranks and where you could hit a ceiling.

Group life and disability benefits: This is life assurance that is taken out in case you die or become disabled. You or your dependants are the beneficiaries of any claim. These benefits are normally part of your retirement fund benefits. The assurance cover is effective both when you are at work and at home.

Leave (holidays): Leave comes in a number of different forms, including:

- Annual leave: Annual leave can vary depending on the job you hold. Annual leave normally varies between 15 and 20 working days a year (or three weeks to four weeks). If public holidays fall within the period you are on leave, the days are often added to your leave. Your contract should tell you the period in which you must take your leave. If you are unable to take leave owing to work circumstances, you should establish the alternatives. For example, will you be paid out in lieu of leave, or will you be able to defer it to the following year's leave cycle?
- Accumulated leave: Many companies allow you to accumulate five working days or one week a year. This is a useful perk as you can build up leave to take an extended overseas holiday. It is also a useful insurance policy in case you lose your job for whatever reason. You will be paid out for your accumulated leave when you leave. (You will be taxed on this amount.)

This money could be used to sustain you until you find another job. Most companies place a limit on the number of days you may accumulate. The maximum is normally about 60 working days (three months).

- Sick leave: You will normally be given a fixed number of days of sick leave at full pay, and further days at reduced pay.
- Maternity and paternity leave: Women often receive three months or more in leave, and fathers about a week. This leave may be paid or unpaid.
- Compassionate leave: Many companies give about seven days a year in leave for when there is a family trauma, such as the death of a close relative. This is normally paid leave.

Holiday allowances: These allowances used to be quite common but are fast disappearing. Normally they are structured with both you and your employer contributing a certain amount every month.

Holiday property owned by the company: Many larger employers, including some government departments, keep holiday properties at the coast, in the Drakensberg or near a game park. They will often offer these facilities to staff members at a reduced rate or for free.

Home loan or mortgage bond assistance: Many larger companies offer some form of home loan assistance. The company may also allow you to make loans against your retirement fund (which is not a good idea, because you reduce your retirement fund benefits); allow you to use your retirement fund savings as security against a home loan from a bank; provide you with a home loan (in very rare circumstances); subsidise your interest payments (within certain limits). There are normally quite a few conditions, including having to work for the company for a certain number of years before you qualify for assistance. Many companies also negotiate deals with banks to get their employees preferential home loan rates.

Hours of work: This is important if you hold a job where overtime is paid. However, in most jobs the working hours tend to be flexible. The intention is that you should work for a minimum number of hours a week. Most jobs nowadays are based on an eight-hour day (including lunch) and a five-day week. This is, however, not cast in stone. Many employers look with favour on people who are prepared to put in extra hours of overtime when the pressure is on. This does not mean that you should be at work at 5 am every day and leave after the boss goes home. You should not, however, be intimidated into working long hours on an ongoing basis without being paid for doing so, particularly at lower levels of authority. You are protected by the Basic Conditions of Employment Act, which sets down conditions for overtime work.

Medical aid: Most employers make it obligatory to join a medical aid fund to which both you and your employer will share contributions.

Membership of a professional organisation or employee organisation (including a trade union): It is against the law for anyone to force you to join any employee or professional organisation. It is equally against the law to prevent you from joining any legal organisation. It is also illegal for an employer to put pressure on you not to join an organisation, for example, by saying you would ruin your job prospects.

The only organisations that you can be forced to join are professional associations such as the Law Society if you are a lawyer, or the Medical and Dental Council if you are a medical doctor. Being a member is part of the condition of being allowed to do the job, no matter who employs you, or whether you are self-employed. This is to keep unsavoury and unqualified people out of the professions.

Before joining any workplace organisation, carefully read its constitution and understand its aims and objectives. Remember that workplace organisations can benefit you enormously. The type of things they do is to negotiate for better working conditions, including pay; to provide assistance if you are in trouble; to protect you from any unfair employment practice; to negotiate severance packages if the company lays off employees; and often to help in improving your work skills.

Overtime: If you are being paid for overtime work, the amounts should be set down in your contract or in an agreement with an employees' association or union for working extra hours on an ordinary working day, public holidays and Sundays. If overtime is not set down in your contract it could also be covered by the Employment Equity Act, which requires people below a certain level who earn less than a fixed amount, to be paid overtime based on their basic income.

Pay or remuneration: This will include the amount you will be paid, how it will be paid (monthly or weekly) and how any increases may be structured.

Retirement fund: Most employers make it obligatory for you to join a retirement fund to which both you and your employer will contribute. You will probably be given more than one choice. There are four basic retirement fund vehicles used for the build-up of retirement savings that are recognised in law. These are:

- **Defined benefit pension funds.** With a defined benefit fund your employer takes the risk that you will be paid a pension at a rate that is agreed upon when you start working for that employer. The term 'defined benefit' means just that: a benefit (pension) that is agreed upon (defined) on the day that you start work. Defined benefit does not mean that the employer will pay you what you need – only the amount agreed upon on the day you started work. Your pension will be based on how much you are earning at retirement and the number of years you have worked for your employer. Your employer takes the risk that there will be enough money to pay you the pension you are promised. Very few employers now offer defined benefit funds because of the risk that they may have to pay in extra money. When you reach retirement you can take up to one-third as a lump sum. The rest of the money must be used to buy a monthly pension. Both you and your employer contribute to the fund on the basis of a percentage of your salary.
- **Defined contribution pension funds** (also known as money purchase funds). With defined contribution funds your employer agrees to put a fixed amount into your retirement savings every month. Whether you have enough money by the time you retire is your problem, not your employer's. These funds are called defined contribution funds because the contribution made by both you and your employer is stated when you start work. You take the risk that you will have enough money for your retirement years. When you reach retirement, you can take up to one-third as a lump sum. The rest of the money must be used to buy a monthly pension.
- **Defined contribution provident funds.** A defined contribution provident fund works in the same way as a defined contribution pension fund, but at retirement you may take the entire amount as a lump sum. However, you lose certain tax benefits in the build-up of your retirement

savings, particularly as you are not able to deduct your contributions from your taxable income.

- **Retirement annuity funds.** Smaller employers will often offer to pay part of your contributions to a retirement annuity fund. Retirement annuities are similar to a defined contribution fund. The major difference is that it is a fund managed by a life assurance company. You cannot withdraw any money from a retirement annuity until the age of 55. When you do withdraw the money, you have to use two-thirds to buy an annuity (a monthly pension). You can take the other one-third as a lump sum.

   As with defined contribution and defined benefit pension funds, you can deduct your contributions, within fixed limits, from tax. This means you defer your tax on the money until you retire. When you retire, the tax is worked the same way as for defined contribution and defined benefit retirement funds.

   Retirement annuity funds can also be used by people who are self-employed, in order to save for retirement.

When you change jobs you should always preserve your retirement savings. If you do not, you are very unlikely to have sufficient money when you reach retirement age. The money will also be taxed if you withdraw it before retirement age. You have a number of options to preserve your retirement savings. These are:

- Defer your pension: You may be able to remain a member of the existing fund if the fund rules allow for this. You will then become what is called a deferred pensioner. When you reach retirement age in terms of the rules of the fund, you take normal retirement. There are no tax consequences and no reinvestment costs that can come to more than the 6 percent of your accumulated retirement savings.
- Transfer to a new sponsored fund: The rules of most employer-sponsored funds allow you to transfer your accumulated retirement savings from a previous sponsored fund to a new sponsored fund of which you may become a member. There will be no tax consequences and there will be no reinvestment costs.
- Transfer to a retirement annuity or a preservation fund: As with a deferred pension and a transfer to a new sponsored fund there are no immediate tax consequences, but there are other consequences, particularly costs, which must not be underestimated. Costs can be as high as 6 or 7 percent when you invest, and then up to 2.5 percent a year thereafter. You should

only consider these two options if the deferred pension or transfer to a new sponsored fund is not available to you. Both vehicles are designed to 'warehouse' your retirement savings until you retire.

The main features of a retirement annuity are:

- the money is tied up at least until you are 55;
- you will not be able to make any withdrawals or take out loans against your savings before 55; and
- you have the option of keeping the money in the fund until the age of 69, at which age you must use the money to draw a pension.

When you mature your retirement annuity you must use at least two-thirds of the accumulated capital to purchase an annuity (a pension), and you can make additional contributions to the fund on a regular or ad hoc basis.

The main features of a preservation fund are:

- you get both pension and provident preservation funds (if you are transferring from a defined benefit or defined contribution pension fund, you must transfer to a pension preservation fund, and if you are a member of a provident fund you must transfer to a provident preservation fund);
- the retirement age of the preservation fund is the same as the sponsored fund from which you have transferred your retirement savings;
- you cannot remain a member of a preservation fund past the age of 69;
- you cannot make additional contributions to a preservation fund;
- the length of your membership of the initial fund plus the period of membership of the preservation fund will determine how much of the one-third lump sum will be exempt from tax; and
- you are permitted to make one withdrawal from a preservation fund.

Share options: Share options are offered as an incentive for employees to ensure that the company makes good profits. Share options normally only apply to companies that are listed on the Johannesburg Stock Exchange. They are a form of ownership of the company. If you own shares, you own a part of the company. However, part-ownership of a company is not limited to listed companies.

You may also be offered a share of a privately owned company for many different reasons, and if you are in a profession such as accountancy or law and you work for a partnership, you are likely, after a number of years, to be offered a partnership. If you are given a partnership you still receive your salary, as well as a share of the overall profits.

Share options are increasingly used as a tool to encourage employee interest in and loyalty to a company. In some companies all employees are offered share options no matter what their seniority. The number of shares, however, is likely to be very small in this case. The significant share options are offered to key staff or senior management whom the company does not want to lose. Share options play a significant role in South Africa because of the shortage of highly skilled and well-trained people, particularly at senior managerial level.

Share options come in many different forms and can have different tax consequences. Most take the form of employees being offered shares at a fixed price. They can then buy the shares in packages over a number of years. For example, for the first two years they may not take up any options, but after five years they may take up all the options. Share options only work when the share price of the company goes up. When you take up a share option you pay the original price at what it was offered to you. You can then sell the share at the higher price, taking the profit and paying tax on the profit.

Subsistence allowances: These allowances are paid to people who are required to be away from home in other towns or countries to do their jobs. The allowances can take different forms. All your costs could be paid; you could be given a set allowance; or there may be a combination of paying actual costs and an allowance. There are tax-free limits on the different combinations of allowances.

Time off: If you are not paid overtime but are expected to work extra hours, particularly on public holidays and weekends, there will normally be a structure for time off in compensation. In terms of the law you are entitled to time off or additional payment for working extra time.

Training: Training is becoming an essential part of any employment package. Technology is developing so rapidly that you will never keep up or get ahead in your career without ongoing training. Any training that is offered to you should be grabbed with both hands, particularly if your employer is paying. Additional education and training is both to your advantage and your employer's.

Many employers are willing, within certain conditions, to pay for additional training and to give you time off to be trained, particularly if it makes you a more productive employee.

Many employers conduct in-house training in a number of ways. Senior and experienced staff may be used to train others, or outside experts may be called in. This type of training is nearly always free for you.

If you want additional training or education outside your place of employment, the employer will often agree to pay, but with conditions. The normal condition is that your employer will lend you the money, which you must start paying back immediately on a monthly basis. However, when you pass the course or sections of the course you are reimbursed.

Unemployment benefits: There are benefits should you lose your job, but they are not provided by your employer, unless you are made redundant (your company is not firing you because you have been incompetent or dishonest, but simply because they no longer need your skills). If you are made redundant you will be offered what is called a redundancy package, which normally means you leave with a minimum of one week's pay for every year of employment. This benefit, however, is unlikely to be listed in your employment contract.

The government manages a fund called the Unemployment Insurance Fund (UIF). Membership of the fund is compulsory. One percent of your pay goes towards the UIF, with an equal amount being contributed by your employer. If you lose your job for whatever reason, you can then claim 45 percent of the salary you were earning when you lost your job. You may only claim assistance from the fund for a maximum of 26 weeks.

Often trade unions also have limited unemployment funds to help members until they can find a new job.

Unsocial hours: Often companies that keep going 24 hours a day, such as factories, mines and even hotels, as well as government departments, such as the police and hospitals, will pay additional money for night shifts or over weekends. This may also apply where you have to start work very early in the morning before public transport is available.

Workers' compensation: This is assurance provided by the government, which pays out if you are temporarily or permanently injured or develop an occupational disease (such as lung damage from handling asbestos) as a direct result of your occupation. Every employer who has more than one employee must register and pay contributions to the Workers' Compensation Fund. You do not pay any contributions.

OTHER ISSUES
A number of other issues also affect your employment.

LABOUR DISPUTES

There are very strict legal requirements about how a labour dispute must be handled. Labour law is very complex, with many books written on the issue. This is only a basic guide on the procedures that must be followed by both you and your employer.

Your grievance

If you have a dispute with your employer that cannot be resolved, there are procedures that you must follow. The first thing that you need to understand is that disputes can fall into two areas. If you do not like the positioning of your desk, that is a complaint you have about a situation that you need to attempt to resolve with your immediate superior. However, if the difference of opinion is over something in your contract, or which is contrary to labour law, then you have a grievance.

Most companies have a set grievance procedure, which follows a number of steps. You may and can involve any employee organisation representative or a labour lawyer to help you with your grievance. The union help would come for free, but you would have to pay a labour lawyer.

Here is a broad outline of the steps to follow:

- Step One: Informal discussion with your immediate superior. If no resolution is obtained you move to step two.
- Step Two: A formal letter stating the details of your grievance. This could result in a number of things, including a meeting with senior members of management. If there is still no agreement you then proceed to the next step.
- Step Three: Submission of the dispute to an independent third party to arbitrate. This can be within or outside the mechanisms of the Commission for Conciliation, Mediation and Arbitration, which was established in terms of the Labour Relations Act and approved by Parliament in 1995.

- Step Four: If there is a serious grievance, the issue can also be taken to the Labour Court, where a finding can be made on whether an unfair labour practice exists.

Apart from the above steps you are also entitled to sue your employer in the civil courts for an unfair labour practice.

Disciplinary measures against you

If your employer is dissatisfied with something you have done and wants to discipline or fire you, there is a process that must be followed. Different employers will have different procedures, some of which may have been compiled in negotiation with employee organisations. All procedures should follow these broad steps:

- Step One: If an employer is dissatisfied with something you have done or not done, you should first be advised verbally and counselled about the unacceptable behaviour. If the problem is of a gross nature, such as theft or assault of a co-worker, this step could be skipped. Your employer or supervisor would have to tell you about the nature of the complaint, provide evidence of your perceived wrongful acts and explain what will happen in the future if you do not modify your behaviour.
- Step Two: Written warnings are issued to you.
- Step Three: You must appear at a disciplinary hearing. At this stage the situation is serious. A hearing could hand down various punishments, from suspension from work to dismissal.

If you feel you have been unjustly dismissed you can then declare a dispute and take the issue to the Commission for Conciliation, Mediation and Arbitration. Your complaint must be made within 30 days of the alleged unfair labour practice. If the dispute cannot be resolved by conciliation, it will be referred to the Labour Court.

8

Your Own Business

A better heading for this chapter may have been 'Creating your own Job'. Your own business is increasingly the only future for many young people. The reason is that the South African job market shrunk by hundreds of thousands of jobs between 1990 and 2002.

This means that young people coming into the job market will not find work unless they have skills that are particularly in demand. And even if you do find a job you will have no guarantee that it is for life. Gone are the days when you were loyal to your employer and your employer was loyal to you. The 'job for life' concept is now a very brief part of history. Even though there are tough laws to protect employees, the legislation does not provide any guarantees of job security or that you will have a job for life. When you sign up for a job you must think what will happen if you should lose that job when you are forty and have children to educate.

The other downside of having a job is that it is unlikely to make you wealthy. Only very exceptional employees with exceptional qualifications, who reach the highest level in big companies and are awarded significant options to buy shares cheaply in their company, are ever likely to get really rich.

The chances of getting to be really wealthy are far greater when you own your own business. Look at most of the world's richest people – they own their own businesses. Consider all the people you know, and again you will find that most of those who are financially successful own their own business.

So the answer is to create your own job. People who employ themselves as well as other people are the ones who get really rich. There are big risks involved in being an entrepreneur, but also immense and satisfying rewards. You will have to risk savings, your reputation and the chance of failure, but if you go about it in the right way you will reduce the risk dramatically.

In this chapter you will discover the formula for success. You will find out:

- How to choose the right business
- How to start up a new business
- Why profit is important
- How to draw up a business plan
- How a business is structured
- How to finance your business
- How to keep track of your business
- How to make your business grow

The Ten Steps to Being an Entrepreneur

A business does not simply happen. You must follow ten steps to assess whether you are in a position to open your own business, the type of business you should open and how to make it a going concern. As Alice was told in her journey through Wonderland: 'If you don't know where you are going any road will do.' The ten steps to being an entrepreneur are as follows:

- Assess yourself
- Personal finances
- Identify your skills
- Market research
- A business plan
- Your resources
- Your financial plan
- Your business ownership structure
- Business ownership choices
- Revisiting your start-up plans

ASSESS YOURSELF

You need to take a long, hard look at yourself and your situation in order to see whether you are capable of putting into the business the financial, emotional and psychological commitment that is required for success. You need to honestly consider a number of factors that affect your personal life, which have nothing or very little to do with the management of a business, but everything to do with your commitment to running a business.

The factors you need to consider include:

SELF-SACRIFICE

Your own business will require a great deal of commitment and hard work. Ask yourself whether:

- You are prepared to work long hours, seven days a week.
- You are willing to forgo holidays, maybe for many years.
- You want to give up many of the pleasures you may now enjoy, from sports activities to entertainment.
- You want to pitch up at the office even when you are feeling ill and exhausted.

SELF-RESPONSIBILITY

Unlike when you have a job and your employer takes care of many aspects of your personal affairs, you will have to take responsibility for yourself. These responsibilities include:

- Paying taxes: You have to arrange to pay your taxes. This includes ensuring that you set aside enough money every month to be able to pay your tax bill when it arrives. You no longer have an employer doing this for you.
- Healthcare: You will need to arrange medical cover for yourself, your dependants and any employees.
- Retirement: You will not automatically have a retirement scheme provided by an employer. You will have to arrange and pay for your retirement savings plan. And remember, you have no employer subsidising contributions to either your retirement fund or medical aid. *You* are now the employer!

- Income: In a nine-to-five job, your salary at the end of the month is guaranteed. When you run your own business, it is not. In bad months, you may not be able to pay yourself as much as you would like or have planned. Yet, you will still have to pay all your bills, feed your family, pay the running costs of your business and put petrol in your car.

YOUR FAMILY

If you have a dependent family, you will need to take them into account. You need to ask how running your own business will affect your family life. Will you be able to work from home, or will you be away from home for long periods? Will your family help in running the business? Will they provide the moral support you will need?

YOUR PERSONAL FINANCES

Your personal finances must be in order. If you cannot meet the following requirements, then you should delay starting your own business until you can get yourself sorted out. The factors to consider are:

PERSONAL DEBT

If you have no personal debt your position is immediately strengthened. You will then be starting a business without any financial demands being made to cover your personal debt repayments. It will also be easier for you to borrow money (and at cheaper rates) to cover any start-up capital and cash flow problems you may encounter. The early failure of many a business is often the result of over-ambitious plans and insufficient capital to keep it going in the short term.

PROTECTION AGAINST THE UNEXPECTED

If you run your own business and you are in a car crash that leaves you incapacitated for six months, you should have a plan for how you and – if you have a family – your spouse and children will survive during the period when you will not be able to generate money. You should speak to a good financial adviser about such things as life assurance and income protection plans. Income protection plans come in different forms and your monthly premiums can vary, depending on the length of the period you are able to sustain yourself before you require the income plan to kick in. Generally, the longer the period that you can afford to sustain yourself before you would require an income protection plan to kick in, the cheaper your premiums will be.

IDENTIFY YOUR SKILLS

The first principle of starting a business is to stick to what you know best. While there are exceptions, this is generally a pretty good guideline for success. If you are good at electronics, you have a far better chance of making a success as an electrician with your own company than as a tour guide competing with Ferdi's company (of *Big Brother* fame). You need to take great care before you venture into a line of business about which you know very little.

You should list all your skills and interests and do a rough assessment of whether you can use any of them to make a success of running a business.

The skills you have can come from many areas. You probably have more skills than you realise. Even managing your own personal finances properly is a skill that will contribute towards running a successful business.

Sources of skills include:

- **Past employment experience:** This could be built up from many years in a job, or from working during vacations while at school or university. You should list every job experience you have had, no matter how brief.
- **Education:** The better educated you are, the greater your chances of success. Anyone starting off as an entrepreneur should consider doing at least one course that provides the basics in running a business.
- **Hobbies:** Many a successful business has grown out of a hobby. Hobbies, because your interest and commitment are voluntary, are often a good place to start. If you are keenly interested in something you are more likely to succeed.

- **Interests:** Many people build up substantial skills because of outside interests. Interests could range from being the treasurer of the school parents' association through to organising the sports club at work.

You will probably require additional training to acquire all the skills you need. Any money you spend investing in your own skills will probably provide you with the best investment return you will get.

Don't rush off to the first course you see advertised. Consider the skills you have already. Speak to friends who are running their own businesses and find out what skills they had to acquire and what they did to get the skills.

MARKET RESEARCH

Once you have identified the various areas in which your particular skills could contribute to a successful business, you need to establish whether there is actually a need for that type of business. Establishing a need is simply another way of asking whether there will be a demand for the product or service you intend to provide.

If you are an air-conditioning expert in KwaZulu-Natal, there may be so many air-conditioning experts in the area that there will be little demand for your services. The answer to establishing the right business in the right area is market research.

Market research means establishing whether there will be a demand for your service or product. There are companies that focus on doing market research. Although market research provided by a professional company is expensive, you can often get a cheaper version. Many market research companies do general surveys, and can provide you with information about a particular region that will assist you relatively cheaply.

You can do your own research in a number of ways. One of the easiest is to go door to door in your neighbourhood, or buttonhole shoppers outside a shopping mall asking them whether there is a need for your service or product, and how much people would be prepared to pay. You also need to establish how many other businesses are offering the same product or service in the area where you want to set up your own business.

An example of a market research survey

Proposed Business: Refrigeration & Stove Servicing Company
Details of respondent:
Name:
Address:
Approximate age:

Questions:
1. Have you required refrigeration or stove repair service in the past?
2. How many times?
3. How easy was it to get the service?
4. Was the service done at your home; or was the faulty appliance taken away; or did you have to deliver it to the service facility?
5. Can you recall the nature of the problem?
6. Can you recall how much you paid?
7. Would you be interested in a local service that provides the service in your own home?

Often market research will provide you with the names and addresses of your first customers. You should use any market research that you do as the basis for a data bank of customers and potential customers.

A BUSINESS PLAN

A business plan has one simple objective: to build a business in order to make a profit. Before you start any business venture you need to be able to predict whether you will make a profit. You cannot merely guess whether you will make a profit. That is particularly dangerous if you are investing a significant amount of money.

Your business plan, particularly if built on market research, will identify exactly:

- What you want to do
- How you will do it
- Where you will do it
- When you will do it
- With whom you will do it

- What you need to do it
- What it will cost you to do it
- Where you may encounter problems
- Whether you can keep doing it
- Most importantly, for whom (your customers) you will do it.

Among other things, your business plan will:
- Tell you whether your proposed business is viable (i.e. whether you will make a profit).
- Enable you to borrow money to start your business.
- Open up lines of supply, telling you what you must buy, how you will finance your purchases and who your suppliers will be.

After you have launched your business, your business plan will be your strategy document or battle plan that you will use to keep your business going as a profitable venture. It will also be your early warning system, helping you to identify any deficiencies in your original loose plans.

As with many other things, the development of a business plan is a logical process. Altogether there are seven issues with which you must deal.

1. WHERE TO START

You may be able to draw up a business plan on your own, but if you are investing a substantial amount of money in your new venture you will probably be saving yourself time, and eventually a great deal of money, by bringing in some expertise. There are a growing number of companies that specialise in assisting new businesses to get off the ground and to keep going successfully. The cost of getting advice can be quite high, but if it saves you from disaster and preserves your savings it will be well worth it.

If you are not investing significant amounts of money and your intention is to start off as a one-person venture, then you can design your own plan. Many banks have departments that will assist you with your plans, as will organisations such as the Small Business Development Corporation.

Your plan should be concise, understandable and useable. It is not something you are going to draw up once and then forget about.

Always overestimate the challenges but underestimate the rewards. That way you increase the chances of success.

2. DEFINING YOUR BUSINESS

To define your business you need a mission statement, which is nothing more than a statement setting down what your business is going to do, how it is going to do it and for what purpose. A mission statement can be as simple as: 'My business will make superior widgets at the lowest possible price for distribution in my neighbourhood.' It can also be a lot more complex, setting down such things as ethical standards and basic employee relations. The main objective of a mission statement is for both you and anyone else to understand what your business is about and how it will succeed.

Once you have a mission statement you should, in broad terms, set down your goals. You need to list the following elements:

- **The business:** What products and/or services your business will provide. This should contain a full description of all the elements.
- **The processes:** How the products and/or services will be manufactured and provided. This should be detailed. If technology is involved, all the procedures and elements should be described.
- **The skills:** What skills you have, what skills you need and how you will obtain the required skills that you do not have.
- **The place:** The accommodation you need now and in the future.
- **The equipment:** The equipment you have and will need.
- **The business structure:** The legal business structure is important, particularly if more than one of you owns the business.

3. KNOW THE COMPETITION

Very seldom, and increasingly less so, will you be the only one in your field of endeavour. Even if you do come up with something really new and unique, it will not be long before someone is copying you or producing something very similar. Unless you know and understand what your competition is doing, you have very little chance of having a successful outsmarting strategy.

There are a number of factors you need to establish. These include:

Competitors: You need to compile a list of all the other companies doing the same type of business in the same area in which you want to do business. You should also consider the possibility of other, already established businesses in other regions moving into the same territory as you.

Competitive advantage: Every business needs to have a competitive advantage if it is to succeed. The best competitive advantage is a monopoly where you have no competition, but that is a bit difficult to organise. By identifying the competitive edge of competitors you will know what you need to do to compete successfully with them. Most competitive advantage is based on one or more of the following:

- **Quality:** This can be the quality of service or the product. Obviously the better the product, the more expensive it is likely to be.
- **Price:** The price of many mass-market goods, such as soap powder, will often be the deciding factor.
- **Follow-up service:** Often if someone knows that they can get good and reliable follow-up service, they will purchase that product.
- **Branding:** Name recognition, particularly built on a combination of the above factors, will provide the edge.

4. YOUR MARKETING PLAN

Marketing is a multifaceted operation. Successful marketing is: providing the right products or services that people need at the right time, at the right place, at the right price and at a profit.

Or, put another way: the elements of marketing can be described as the Five Ps. They are:

- Production
- Price
- Promotion
- Place
- Profit

The failure of many businesses is that they only get one or two of the marketing elements right. You will not make many sales if you produce great widgets but do not get them to where people can buy them; or manage to convince people why they should buy them; or tell them where they can buy them; or if they are not priced correctly.

Successful marketing has three stages. These are:

- **Planning:** Planning includes the setting of objectives, evaluating opportunities, drawing up marketing strategies and marketing plans, and developing a marketing programme.

- **Implementation:** Implementation does not mean starting to produce the product or service, but implementing the entire plan or programme from production to final sale.
- **Control:** You need to constantly measure the success of your plan and adapt it as conditions change. This includes a constant evaluation of your entire marketing plan.

Each element of marketing, from the start of the process through to the final sale, must be carefully planned, implemented and controlled, taking account of five elements:

1. Production

Production is the foundation stone on which all else is built. You need to define your production processes very carefully in your business plan, particularly the quality control measures. Production has a number of important parts. These include:

- **Right product or service.** You need to base this on your market research and not on providing something that merely entertains you.
- **Features.** You must have a clear idea of what will make your product or service different from your competitors'. This may include a number of issues, from the way you package your product or service through to design. Design is a complex issue, ranging from choice of colour through to shape. You may find that you need to call in outside expertise to ensure that you can produce an aesthetically pleasing product.
- **Premises and equipment.** To provide a product or service, you must have the correct equipment and premises. The choice of the right premises and equipment must be properly planned, costed and installed. You should also keep in mind future expansion.
- **Production line plan.** You must have a clearly defined plan for the management of the production process, from the purchase of any primary materials through to the completed article. Your production line plan should preferably be done with what is called a flow chart, showing and defining each step of the process. A production line applies as much to a product as a service. It is the order in which you do things. Among other things, a production line plan helps you to establish how much staff you may need to employ, and the equipment you need to purchase.

- **Quality.** You must produce a service or a product that is reliable and of a good standard. If you produce and sell a product that is faulty or sub-standard, it will soon develop a bad reputation and sales and potential sales will be rapidly undermined, as will your business venture.
- **Guarantees.** You need to decide what guarantees or warranties you will give on your product or service. Many consumers consider a guarantee as essential. Guarantees also help to keep your business focused on quality. Guarantees come in many different forms. They include: life warranties; limited-term warranties, such as one or two years; or parts but not labour warranties.
- **Branding.** Branding means name recognition. If you buy an existing business you will often find that you pay for what is called 'goodwill'. This is essentially what you are paying for a good brand name. It could vary from a corner hardware shop through to a franchise operation. Franchise operations in particular spend substantial amounts of money in building brand recognition. The objective of branding is to convince customers that they will receive consistent quality from your product or service. Branding can mean as much to your corner hardware store as it means to the world's strongest brand, Coca-Cola.

2. Target markets

An unfocused selling campaign, where you see the entire world population as your potential customers, is not likely to succeed. You have to know to whom you are selling your goods and services. For example, there is as little point in attempting to sell antiques in a lower-income area as there is in having a second-hand shoe shop in an upper-income area. Deciding on your customer is absolutely vital to the success of your business. The objective is to keep your distribution costs as low as possible. The basis of targeting your market is what is called market segmentation. Market segmentation is clustering people with similar needs who will respond in much the same way to your product or service.

The first step is to define your target market into a rough segmentation. These segmentations are:

- **Mass-based target market:** This means aiming your service or product at everyone. Coca-Cola is a good example.
- **Broad-based target market:** A broad-based target market is aimed

at specific people with specific needs. For example, disposable nappies are aimed at a very specific group of people.

- **Narrow-based target market:** This could be based on a number of factors. For example, if you are offering refrigeration and stove repair services, you will want to narrow down your area of operation, otherwise you could spend most of your time travelling vast distances and doing little income-generating work.

Common ground is important when you are grouping people by taking a number of similarities into account. These include:

- **Gender:** Some goods and services are specific to the two gender groups, such as magazines for women or baldness cures for men.
- **Income and wealth:** These are important when it comes to producing a product or service that people may not necessarily need but want. The wealthier they are, the likelier they are to spend more on non-essentials. A need is a square meal of chicken, rice and vegetables. A want is caviar and champagne. Needs tend to be cheaper, widely marketed commodities, while products or services aimed at fulfilling wants, need to be targeted at specific groups.
- **Needs segmentation:** People in different circumstances need different things, e.g. learners need textbooks.
- **Occupation and education:** Occupation and education determine many needs and wants and, more particularly, affordability.
- **Interests and hobbies:** The wealthier society is in general, the more money they have to spend on interests and hobbies. Interests and hobbies are often the basis of quite wide groups of people (e.g. people with pets is a significant market sector). .
- **Geographical areas:** People living in different areas have different needs. For example, in a high crime area they need better security.
- **Age:** Many products and services are aimed at specific age groups. The broad age groups are youth, young adults, middle-aged adults and, increasingly important, the elderly, retired group.

3. Distribution

You have to get your product or service to the market at the right time in the right numbers and at the right place to achieve sales. Distribution is a complex matter and needs careful planning. Distribution has a number of important elements. These include:

- **Initial storage:** You must have stock in hand to be able to supply retailers or customers. This applies particularly to the provision of products.
- **Transport:** You have to get your product or service to the place where it is required. This can be as simple as buying a bakkie with which to make deliveries, to something as complex as arranging the export of your products to a foreign country. If your products are transported by a third party you need to compare a number of issues, including costs, reliability of service, handling and security.
- **Point of sale:** You need to select the place or places where the sale will be made. The more convenient it is for your customers to access your product or service, the more likely they will be to make a purchase.
- **Costs:** Costs of all stages of distribution need to be assessed and listed.
- **Reliability:** Your distribution service must be reliable. If you say you will deliver by a certain day in the week, you must meet that deadline.
- **Quantity:** Quantity covers a number of different factors. These include: the initial quantity you produce; the quantity you need to store; the additional quantity you may need to produce; and the quantity you need at each place of sale. Remember that the greater the quantity that you have in hand, the higher your costs.
- **Security:** Security has become an increasingly important issue. In most cases the responsibility for security is yours until you have delivered your product or service to the purchaser.
- **Replenishment:** This means having systems in place so that you know when you have to replenish stocks, and being able to supply the replenishments when required.
- **Systems:** There are now computer programs available that will make distribution far more efficient, providing cost and time saving. With the correct computer systems you can keep very accurate track of your inventory (stock). Computers can tell you at the press of a button how much you have in stock, how much is en route and how much is at the point of sale. Increasingly, retailers are installing computer systems that are connected to their suppliers and that enable automatic orders for replenishment when stocks are running low.

4. Price

Pricing of your product or service is one of the more difficult decisions you will have to make. Pricing will make the difference between making a profit or a loss. Pricing is not simply a matter of deciding on how much you want for your product. It is a balancing act between what you would like to charge and what your customers are prepared to pay.

Price setting is influenced by many factors, including:

- **Input costs:** These are your costs in producing a product or service. These costs range from raw materials to equipment you need in production.
- **Business-operating costs:** These are the everyday costs of running your business, which are not directly related to the production of the service or product. The costs range from office rent to the telephone bill.
- **Capital costs:** These are the costs of setting up your business or buying equipment. Capital costs can be written off over a number of years. The capital cost includes any interest you pay on loans you make to purchase capital equipment.
- **Competition:** The price being charged by your competitors for the same or a similar product or service is a major factor in what you will be able to charge. It is unlikely that you will be able to charge more, unless you can provide something extra that will encourage customers to consider the price as secondary. For example, if you are the owner of a television sales company, you could offer free tuning services with every purchase over a certain amount.
- **Demand and supply:** The greater the demand and the lower the supply, the greater the price. The lower the demand and the greater the supply, the lower the price.
- **Life cycle:** If there is low supply and prices are initially high when a new product or service is launched, other providers are likely to enter the market. The result is that the prices can be expected to fall in the future.
- **Discounts:** If you are providing a product to a retailer, you will have to give various discounts to encourage them to give priority to promoting the sale of your product over others. There are many different types of discounts that can be given. These include: cash discounts for upfront payments; bulk discounts when a customer buys more than a certain number; discounts for favourable promotion; and

loyalty discounts for customers who provide you with solid ongoing business, particularly when the supply is contractual.

After taking all these factors into account you will have to decide on a pricing policy. This could involve having flexible prices. For example, if there is a seasonal demand for your product or service, you will have to lower prices at times of low demand and up them when there is high demand.

5. Promotion

Promotion of your product or service simply means telling people it is there. Promotion can be simple and cheap, or it can involve a multi-million-rand campaign with advertisements in newspapers, magazines, on radio and television.

Promotion can have various targets. These include:

- Encouraging dealers to stock greater numbers of your product.
- Encouraging customers to sample your product or service.
- Encouraging customers to remain loyal to your product or service.
- Combating competition.
- Improving distribution.

There are many ways to tell people about your product or service. These include:

- **Free publicity:** If you can generate media interest in your product you will get free publicity. You should read newspapers and listen to the radio to establish how other companies manage to get free publicity.
- **Display materials at the point of sale:** Often, at a cost, retailers will permit in-store promotions.
- **Awards for sales staff:** Sales staff can be encouraged by the use of incentives to promote your product.
- **Special discounts:** Promotional discounts are a well-used tool for getting people to sample or stay loyal to products and services, e.g. lower prices could be given on the introduction of a product.
- **Demonstrations:** You can give free samples or have demonstrations at the place of sale.
- **Sponsorships:** Sponsorship entails paying all or part of the costs of a community event in return for associating your brand with the event.

- **Advertising:** This is paid promotion of your product or service. Advertising can range from distributing pamphlets in letter boxes to advertising on television.

When advertising, you need to decide on a number of issues. These include:

- **Your objective:** Are you introducing a product or attempting to maintain awareness?
- **Your audience:** You need to decide precisely at whom you are aiming your advertising. It is pointless advertising disposable nappies to pensioners.
- **Your message:** You need to know how you are going to tell the story about your product or service.
- **What is the best media:** You have a fairly wide range of options, from billboards to newspapers to radio, and even television if you are going big time.
- **When and how often:** Timing and frequency are key issues.
- **Your costs:** You need to set a budget for advertising. Advertising costs can vary quite dramatically, even in your local newspaper. You can use the classified advertising sections quite effectively without spending much money. However, if you are spending a lot, you will be best advised to use an advertising agency for their expertise.

YOUR RESOURCES

Your business plan must contain a full list of what you already have at your disposal and what you will need. Your resources list has a number of key elements. These are your financial resources, your skills resources, your equipment resources and raw materials.

- **Your financial resources:** The extent of your financial resources will to a large degree determine the size of your operation. You need to list the capital you have and the capital you are likely to need. Included is the amount of money you will need to borrow. In making an assessment of how much you need to borrow, you should also take account of what interest you will be paying on the money. (More on financing your business on p. 114.)

- **Your equipment resources:** Equipment is likely to be your biggest cost in setting up your business. You need to list everything you need, from heavy equipment for making widgets to office equipment and fittings.
- **Your raw materials:** You need to know your primary source for the supply of raw materials, as well as secondary sources (in case something goes wrong with the primary source); and what you are likely to pay for any materials you may need.
- **Skills resources:** You need to list three skill groupings: the skills you will bring to the business, the skills you require in the business on a permanent basis and the skills you can outsource. You need to list any skills training required.

YOUR FINANCIAL PLAN

Most small businesses fail, particularly in the early stages, because there is not sufficient money to keep them running. What happens is that instead of having a virtuous circle of an ever-growing business, you slide into a vicious downward cycle of cost cutting, with a resultant reduction in service or quality and, ultimately, a loss of sales.

A successful financial plan requires an assessment of all costs involved in the business. You need to take into account initial or set-up costs, future capital expenditure and running costs. It is only with a comprehensive business plan that you will identify most of the costs you will incur. A good financial plan must be conservative. Many people fail because they underestimate how much money they will pay out and overestimate the money they will receive. If you do it the other way around – overestimating the costs and underestimating your income – you will not be as vulnerable to things such as high interest rates, failure of customers to pay the bills and increases in your input costs.

You need to know how much it costs to set up or buy the business, how much money the business is likely to earn and how much you are likely to pay out in costs. If you need to borrow money for your business, your bank will spend most of its time looking at your financial plan. The bank will want to see a realistic assessment of where you are and where you hope to be within 12 months and after a few years.

If you do not have financial skills, you should consider getting expert help. Many banks have small business sections that will provide assistance to budding entrepreneurs, helping you to spot the problem areas as well as the big opportunities. Accountants are the primary source of assistance when drawing up a financial plan, but they will need to see your business plan so that they can get a proper grasp of the figures.

There are seven elements to your financial plan. These are start-up costs, raising capital, a cash flow statement, a projected profit and loss statement, a projected balance sheet, scenario planning based on what could happen under different circumstances and break-even point calculations.

1. START-UP COSTS

Your financial plan must tell you how the start-up costs will be funded and, if the money is borrowed, how it will be repaid. Start-up costs should be considered in different ways, depending on your approach to being an entrepreneur:

New business. For a new business you will have to assess all the different costs according to your marketing plan.

Buying an existing business. There are two elements to buying an existing business. These are:

- Price: The price you pay for an existing business should only be settled after an extensive investigation of the business, and particularly of the reasons for the sale, and its actual value.
- Improvements: You may find that you will have to spend additional money on replacing or bringing in new equipment or systems to make the business more efficient and competitive.

Buying into an existing business. Entrepreneurs buy into existing businesses for two main reasons: they bring in additional required skills and/or capital. When buying an existing business or buying into an existing business, including a franchise, you must still base your assessment on a marketing plan.

If the existing business already has a marketing plan, you must study it carefully, compare it with the actual records of the business and make the necessary revisions.

2. RAISING CAPITAL

By this stage you will have a fairly good idea of how much it will cost you to start your new business venture. The next step is to assess how you will raise the capital required. There are three main sources of capital for a business. These are your own savings, investment in your business by others and loans.

- **Your savings:** You need to be careful not to commit your all, in case the business collapses.
- **Other investors:** Other people's money is one of the cheapest forms of money, in that you do not have to repay it or any interest on it. However, you will have to share the profits of the business with your investors. You will have to allocate investors a percentage of shares in your business, and they will receive a percentage of profits in proportion to the number of shares they own. The biggest problem you will have is to convince other people that investment in your business is worthwhile. Many very successful businesses started in this way, with family and friends providing the initial capital. The massive Rembrandt empire of Anton Rupert is a particularly good example.
- **Borrowed money:** Most businesses need loans for start-up capital; to expand; to replace equipment and machinery; and for day-to-day operations. The source of capital is mainly from banks, as well as from institutions that assist with the establishment of new ventures. Lenders will want to see your business plan; your commitment (mainly what risk you are taking personally); what other security you can provide to ensure the institution gets its money back; and repayment schedules, which can take a number of forms, such as only paying interest initially and repaying the capital when your business starts to generate profits.

3. A PROJECTED CASH FLOW STATEMENT

A cash flow statement is a flow chart showing how you expect money to be paid out and paid in. Management of your cash flow affects such things as the level of interest you earn or pay. Pick 'n Pay's Raymond Ackerman is the king of cash flow management. Much of the profit made by Raymond Ackerman's spectacular Pick 'n Pay supermarket chain does not in fact come from what you pay for your groceries – it comes from proper cash flow management. In simple terms, Pick 'n Pay orders goods from its suppliers, which it puts onto the supermarket shelves and sells as quickly as possible for cash. Mr Ackerman then invests the money you have paid. He holds on to the investment for three months and then pays the supplier. In effect, Mr Ackerman does not allow you to buy on credit, but gets 90 days' credit from his suppliers. By using this management of cash flow, Pick 'n Pay can cut the prices on its products to the minimum, and does so knowing that it can generate sufficient profit from the millions it has invested.

However, most businesses do not have it so good. The inflows and outflows are often irregular, requiring short-term borrowings.

With a projected cash flow chart you need a complete list of all your expenditure and income, and the dates of payment for a 12-month period. Look at the top three lines of our cash flow statement. Except for the first month, every month shows a profit. However, if you took only what you sold at the cost of producing those sales into account to calculate whether you are running a successful business, you could soon be in trouble. There are a number of reasons why your net sales figures will not be reflected in your bank balance. The reasons include:

- **Debtors:** Although you may have sold the goods you may still be waiting for payment, while you have had to pay up for the raw materials that you used to make your widgets.
- **Other costs:** Every business has a whole range of costs that is not directly related to the production of your widgets. There are many other costs in running a business, from paying the tea lady through to rent on your offices.

A shortage of cash in the bank can have a number of causes. In the start-up of your business you can expect that money will go out faster than it will come in. But even after you are well along the road to managing a successful business, you may again run into cash flow problems. Reasons can include:

- **Large once-off payments:** You may receive a large bill, such as for tax, which places short-term stress on your bank balance.
- **Seasonal sales:** If you have a business, such as in the tourism trade, that does well at certain times of the year and badly at others, you could well experience cash flow problems in lean months.

PROJECTED CASH FLOW STATEMENT

	Jan	Feb	Mar	April	May	June	July	Aug	Sept	Oct	Nov	Dec	Total
Sales	R80,000	R140,000	R160,000	R170,000	R170,000	R165,000	R165,000	R160,000	R170,000	R180,000	R180,000	R160,000	R1,900,000
Purchases	R132,000	R12,000	R12,000	R132,000	R12,000	R12,000	R132,000	R12,000	R12,000	R132,000	R12,000	R12,000	R624,000
Net sales	−R52,000	R128,000	R148,000	R38,000	R158,000	R153,000	R33,000	R148,000	R158,000	R48,000	R168,000	R148,000	R1,276,000
Opening bank balance	R100,000	−R113,000	−R166,000	−R124,000	−R177,000	−R90,000	R17,000	R4,000	R96,000	R188,000	R165,000	R262,000	R314,000
Payment received													
Cash	R20,000	R40,000	R45,000	R50,000	R40,000	R45,000	R45,000	R45,000	R50,000	R50,000	R50,000	R25,000	R505,000
Debtors	R0	R0	R90,000	R110,000	R140,000	R155,000	R155,000	R140,000	R135,000	R140,000	R140,000	R120,000	R1,325,000
Subtotal	R20,000	R40,000	R135,000	R160,000	R180,000	R200,000	R200,000	R185,000	R185,000	R190,000	R190,000	R145,000	R1,830,000
Payments made													
Wages	R35,000	R35,000	R35,000	R35,000	R35,000	R35,000	R35,000	R35,000	R35,000	R35,000	R35,000	R35,000	R420,000
Loan repayments	R6,000	R6,000	R6,000	R6,000	R6,000	R6,000	R6,000	R6,000	R6,000	R6,000	R6,000	R6,000	R72,000
Office expenses	R10,000	R10,000	R10,000	R10,000	R10,000	R10,000	R10,000	R10,000	R10,000	R10,000	R10,000	R10,000	R120,000
Rent	R14,000	R14,000	R14,000	R14,000	R14,000	R14,000	R14,000	R14,000	R14,000	R14,000	R14,000	R14,000	R168,000
Water, lights	R11,000	R11,000	R11,000	R11,000	R11,000	R11,000	R11,000	R11,000	R11,000	R11,000	R11,000	R11,000	R132,000
Raw materials	R132,000	R12,000	R12,000	R132,000	R12,000	R12,000	R152,000	R12,000	R12,000	R132,000	R12,000	R12,000	R624,000
Sundries	R5,000	R5,000	R5,000	R5,000	R5,000	R5,000	R5,000	R5,000	R5,000	R5,000	R5,000	R5,000	R60,000
Subtotal	R213,000	R93,000	R93,000	R213,000	R93,000	R93,000	R213,000	R93,000	R93,000	R213,000	R93,000	R93,000	R1,596,000
Surplus/shortfall	−R193,000	−R53,000	R42,000	−R53,000	R87,000	R107,000	−R13,000	R92,000	R92,000	−R23,000	R97,000	R52,000	R234,000
Closing bank bal.	−R113,000	−R166,000	−R124,000	−R177,000	−R90,000	R17,000	R4,000	R96,000	R188,000	R165,000	R262,000	R314,000	R548,000

4. PROJECTED PROFIT AND LOSS (OR INCOME AND EXPENDITURE) STATEMENT

A profit and loss statement is simply a list of all the income that will come into your business from sales and all the costs you will pay. By subtracting the costs from the income you will know whether you will make a profit or a loss.

You should draw up a projected profit and loss statement for at least the first 12 months, based on the costs you expect to experience and the sales you expect to make. If possible, you should also attempt to look about two to three years ahead. Your projected profit and loss statement will tell you very quickly whether you have a viable business proposition or not. Your marketing plan will provide the basis for your projected profit and loss statement.

Again, you must be conservative with the figures, overestimating costs and underestimating sales. For example, a hike in interest rates could see your costs going up if you have borrowed money and sales dropping, as customers will also have higher interest bills, which will result in them having less to spend.

When you calculate costs you must take everything into account, right down to how much you will spend on tea and coffee. The capital you bring into your business, whether from your savings or from a loan, is not included in your profit and loss statement, but any interest you pay on a loan must be included, as that is a cost to the business.

Example of a projected profit and loss statement

COMPANY NAME:

Income statement for the year ending ....

Sales		**R**
Less Cost of Sales		
Discounts, etc.	R	
Stock (opening stock plus		
purchases, minus closing stock)	R	
Subtotal		**R**
Gross Profit		**R**
Less Expenses		
Wages	R	
Rent	R	
Office expenses	R	
Advertising	R	
Insurance	R	
Interest	R	
Bank charges	R	
Transport	R	
Repairs and maintenance	R	
Bad debts	R	
Depreciation	R	
Water, electricity	R	
Telephone	R	
Subtotal		**R**
Net Profit/Loss (before tax)		**R**
Less Tax:		**R**
Net Profit/Loss (after tax)		**R**

5. PROJECTED BALANCE SHEET

A projected balance sheet is a statement of how much you expect to owe, how much you expect to own and how much you expect you will be owed in 12 months' time. Or, put in more formal terms, it is a statement of your assets and liabilities and the value of the capital or money invested by shareholders. If your assets exceed your liabilities your business is a going concern. If your liabilities exceed your assets you are bankrupt.

Assets

Assets (the things owned by your business) are separated into three groups. There are fixed assets, non-current assets and current assets. On a balance sheet, assets are normally listed under the heading 'Employment of Capital'. In other words, how is the money invested in the business being put to work in buying profit-producing assets?

- **Fixed assets:** These are assets that are considered permanent and long term. Fixed assets include property, motor vehicles and plant and equipment.
- **Non-current assets:** These assets are long-term investments, but not fixed assets such as property. They include things such as investments made by the company.
- **Current assets:** These assets are likely to be used up within 12 months in the running of the business. Current assets include stock (raw materials already bought, products being manufactured, completed-but-not-sold products and any material used in manufacturing the product), money owed to the business and cash in the bank.

Liabilities

Liabilities (the money owed by your business) are separated into three groups. These are: the investments of the shareholders' or owners' capital; long-term loans; and current liabilities. On a balance sheet, liabilities are normally listed under the heading 'Capital Employed' – in other words, the money available with which to buy assets.

- **Owners' capital:** The money invested by owners is a liability. In effect, this is money that is owed to the owners. It is not only money paid into the business, but also any profits (dividends) not paid to owners, known as retained profits.
- **Long-term liabilities:** These liabilities are mainly long-term loans used to establish the business.
- **Short-term (current) liabilities:** These liabilities are short-term commitments, such as accounts that you have to pay, any bank overdraft or other short-term loan, and tax owed.

Example of a projected balance sheet

ASSETS (Employment of Capital)			LIABILITIES (Capital Employed)		
Fixed Assets			**Owners' Capital**		
Property		R500 000	Owners' initial capital	R500 000	
			Plus: Accumulated		
Machinery	R300 000		profit	R250 000	
Equipment	R100 000		**Total Owners' Capital**		R 750 000
Vehicles	R450 000				
Subtotal	R850 000				
Less: 20%	R170 000	R680 000			
depreciation					
Total Fixed Assets		R1 180 000			
Non-Current Assets			**Long-Term Liabilities**		
36-Month bank deposit	R100 000		SBDC Loan	R350 000	
Employee housing loan	R200 000		Loan from Family	R400 000	
			Trust		
Total Non-Current Assets		R 300 000	**Total Long-Term Liabilities**		R 750 000
Current Assets			**Current Liabilities**		
Stock	R250 000		Creditors (Money	R 30 000	
			owed by business)		
Debtors (Money	R110 000		Tax	R200 000	
owed to business)					
Cash-in-the-bank	R 50 000		Overdraft	R 80 000	
Total Current Assets		R 410 000	**Total Current Liabilities**		R 390 000
TOTAL ASSETS		R1 890 000	**TOTAL LIABILITIES**		R1 890 000

6. SCENARIO PLANNING

Now that you have drawn up your projected cash flow, balance sheet and profit and loss statements, you need to stress test them. Or, put another way, you have to ask the question 'What if?' By doing so, you will see how much tolerance your plans have. You will see what will happen in the best of times as well as in the worst of times.

Most 'What ifs' apply to what are called 'variables' in your business. These are issues that you cannot control, as opposed to things you can control. For example, you can control salaries, but you cannot control interest rates.

There are many 'What ifs'. They include:

- What if interest rates go up or down? If interest rates are low, you need to calculate what effect they would have if they went up by one, 2, 3, 4 and even 5 percent. You can also calculate the upside of interest rates coming down.
- What if the inflation rate goes up or down? Inflation can have a significant effect on your business. You must not only work on the average inflation rate, but also inflation in your particular business, taking account of both input costs and selling prices.
- What happens if the price of your raw materials increases? For example, an increase in the petrol price may have a serious impact on the cost of supplies.
- What if the business burns down? You must have a plan for unexpected disasters. They can range from a major breakdown in production to a three-day strike. The strike may not necessarily be in your business, but could be at the factory of one of your suppliers.
- What if the economy slows down? A slow down in the economy could have a significant impact on your sales.

You need three basic scenarios to show investors and institutions from which you may want to borrow money. These are:

- A best-case scenario: However, you must still be realistic.
- An average scenario: This is what you conservatively and realistically expect to happen.
- A worst-case scenario: Be realistic, taking into account probable problems.

7. THE BREAK-EVEN POINT CALCULATION

A break-even point is the point at which you have made sufficient sales to cover all your costs. It is the point at which your business will make neither a loss nor a profit. Again, this calculation should be conservative.

The break-even point calculation should be used when you do your scenario planning, as it will show in various circumstances whether your business has a better-than-average chance of survival. You will also know how much you must produce and sell before you can make a profit.

The formula to calculate the break-even point is quite simple:

$$\text{Break even} = \frac{\text{Total Expenses} \times 100}{\text{Gross Profit}}$$

Computers have become an essential part of any business and are particularly useful in scenario planning and calculating break-even points. Other advantages of computers are:

- Accuracy: If the correct program and formulae are used, the calculations you require to be made will always be accurate.
- Cost saving: You can now do many of the calculations yourself, which previously required accountants.
- Time saving: Calculations that previously took hours can now be done at the press of a button.

The key programme for business calculations is called a spreadsheet. It is essential that you have a sound knowledge of how spreadsheets work.

YOUR BUSINESS OWNERSHIP STRUCTURE

There are four basic legal structures through which you can own your business, either alone or in association with other investors. Choices for legal structures in business are: a sole proprietorship, a partnership, a close corporation or a company.

SOLE PROPRIETORSHIP

This is the simplest structure. It means a business with one owner, which effectively trades in the name of the owner. The main features of a sole proprietorship are:

- **It is yours:** There is no difference between your personal affairs and your business affairs. For tax purposes you are treated as a single entity.
- **Few registration formalities:** Apart from any local government by-laws, there are no arduous registration procedures or registration formalities.
- **You are liable:** If anything goes wrong with your business, you will be responsible. In other words, your creditors can claim any assets in your name, from your home to your television set.
- **Few responsibilities:** You don't have to get involved with an endless set of professionals providing you with legal advice or having to audit your books. However, you do need to know how to keep records in order to keep track of your business.

A PARTNERSHIP

A partnership is, in some ways, similar to a sole proprietorship. As with a sole proprietorship, the business structure is very informal. It is rather like a number of sole proprietors getting together to run one business. A partnership can be formed on the basis of a number of factors, including investment, skills, ownership of property or labour. If new partners join the business, the existing partnership will have to be dissolved and a new partnership established.

There are two types of partnerships:

- **A normal partnership:** A normal partnership is limited to 20 partners.
- **A professional partnership:** Professional people such as lawyers, architects, medical doctors or engineers often set up partnerships. There is no limit to the number of partners in a professional partnership.

There are a number of advantages to a partnership:

- **No complex registration:** You do not have to register a partnership. However, it is wise to have a partnership agreement setting down the terms of the partnership. The agreement should contain details about the commitments and responsibilities of the various partners.
- **Simple tax:** A partnership is not a separate legal entity, so it is not a taxpayer. The partners are taxed individually as provisional taxpayers according to their share of profits from the partnership.
- **Simple accounting structure:** The income and expenditure of the business are proportionally attributable to each partner.
- **Pools skills and resources:** A partnership is an easy way to bring different skills together and have a larger capital base to improve financial viability.
- **Overcomes problems of sole proprietorship:** In a partnership it is easier to do things such as take time off and even be ill, because you have someone to back you up.

CLOSE CORPORATION

A close corporation is a relatively new business structure. It was introduced to give small business owners some of the protection that shareholders in large companies enjoy, without all the red tape.

The important elements of a close corporation are:

- **Legal standing:** A close corporation (CC) is a legal entity in its own right in terms of the Close Corporations Act. It must be registered with the Registrar of Close Corporations. With registration you need to submit an 'Association Agreement', setting out the terms of the close corporation. A close corporation can both sue and be sued. Unlike a sole proprietorship and a partnership, a close corporation owns its own assets and is responsible for its debts.
- **Limited liability:** Unless it can be shown that you have contravened the Close Corporation Act and have been involved in reckless trading, you cannot be sued in your personal capacity. This means that your liability is limited and your personal assets are protected.
- **Membership:** A close corporation must have at least one member, but not more than 10 members.
- **Administration:** Unlike a company, your financial statements do not need an annual audit, but you are required to produce financial statements once a year. A professional accounting officer must review and sign the statements.
- **Tax:** A close corporation must be registered as a taxpayer with the Receiver of Revenue. It pays company tax on any profits. Profits are distributed to members as tax-free dividends. Secondary tax on companies (STC) is levied on dividends that must be paid by the close corporation. As a close corporation member, you must register as a provisional taxpayer.
- **Perpetual succession:** Unlike a sole proprietorship or partnership, a close corporation continues to exist even if the individual members change or die.

A COMPANY

Companies are established in terms of the Companies Act, which subjects them to fairly strict conditions to operate. There are three main types of company, but all have common features. These include:

- **Registration:** Registration of a company is fairly complex, and you will probably need assistance. Registration is in terms of the Companies Act and requires a memorandum of association and articles of association. The company comes into existence when the Registrar of Companies issues a certificate of incorporation. The memorandum of association gives the general details of the company, including its name, its purpose and the share holdings. The articles of association deal with the internal operations of the company, from board meetings to the powers and responsibilities of a director.

- **Legal standing:** A company is a legal entity in its own right in terms of the Companies Act. A company can both sue and be sued. As with a close corporation, a company owns its own assets and it is responsible for its debts.
- **Limited liability:** Unless it can be shown that you have contravened the Companies Act and have been involved in reckless trading, you cannot be sued in your personal capacity. This means that your liability is limited and your personal assets protected.
- **Administration:** A company must have audited annual statements.
- **Tax:** A company must be registered as a taxpayer with the Receiver of Revenue. A company pays company tax on any profits. Profits are distributed to members as tax-free dividends. Secondary tax on companies (STC) is levied on dividends. As a company director, you must register as a provisional taxpayer (see Chapter 12).
- **Perpetual succession:** As with a close corporation, a company continues to exist even if the individual shareholders change or die.

There are three different types of companies, within which there are some sub-sections. The three different types are: a company without share capital, a private company and a public company.

Companies without share capital

There are two types of companies without share capital, both of which should not make a profit and cannot declare dividends. In its main form, a company without share capital is registered as a Section 21 company. Section 21 companies are used by charities and religious organisations.

A private company

The main features of a private company are:

- Its name must carry the appellation '(Pty) Ltd'.
- It may not offer shares to the public. Any transfer of shares must take place with the approval of the directors.
- There is no minimum number of shareholders, and it may have a minimum of one director.

- The maximum number of shareholders is 50.
- It must have audited annual financial statements, but there is no obligation to publish the statements.
- Shares may be issued at different values. The shares may be issued as ordinary shares, where shareholders have no right to dividends; or preferential shares, where shareholders have a preferential right to dividends, and sometimes capital on liquidation of the company.

A public company

The main features of a public company are:
- The name of the company must end with the word 'Limited'.
- It must have at least seven shareholders and at least two directors.
- It can offer shares to the public.
- It may choose or not choose to be listed on the Johannesburg Stock Exchange.
- It must publish annual audited statements that are available for public perusal.
- Shares may be issued at different values. The shares may be issued as ordinary shares, where shareholders have no right to dividends; or preferential shares, where shareholders have a preferential right to dividends and sometimes capital on liquidation of the company.

BUSINESS OWNERSHIP CHOICES

When you start out as an entrepreneur you essentially have four options of enterprise:

- Starting a business from scratch.
- Buying an existing business.
- Buying into an existing business.
- Buying into a franchise operation.

1. STARTING A NEW BUSINESS

The financial cost of starting your own business will not automatically be lower than buying an existing business. Setting up a new business will cost money. The costs will depend on the initial size of your business and the legal framework you choose. If you are starting out with very little money, it means you will have to start small and gradually build up your business.

The most successful 'greenfield' businesses (new businesses in a new field) are those that are breaking new ground. The best example is in technology. With enormous development taking place in technology, most people with new ideas have little option but to start from scratch. Billionaire Mark Shuttleworth's is a very good example of a greenfield business. He started one of very few businesses involved in Internet security.

2. BUYING AN EXISTING BUSINESS

Buying an existing business can save you a great deal of time and trouble. Advantages of buying an existing business include the following:

- Systems are already in place, from pricing through to the person who makes the morning coffee.
- The business is probably already known (but you need to check that it has a good name).
- It will already have a customer base.
- A network of suppliers will have been built up.
- It will have a trading history, which you should be able to check. This will help you in your own business plan for the business.
- You will not have to spend hours finding premises, furnishings, plant and equipment.

There are eight issues to consider when buying an existing business:

1. Establish the reason for the sale

There can be many reasons for a sale, some good and some bad. You must take time to discover the real reason for the sale. Do not merely accept what you are told. Among other things, you should speak to suppliers and customers. The reasons for the sale can include:

- **Financial problems:** This does not necessarily mean that you are considering buying a bad business. The business could be in trouble because it is undercapitalised.
- **Personal reasons:** These could range from the retirement, relocation or even death of the owner.
- **Changes in market conditions:** Competition may have become increasingly tough, or the competitive edge the owner may previously have had may have been lost. The owner could be attempting to sell at a peak, knowing that a change in market conditions is about to undermine future profitability.

- **It is a lemon:** The business could just be a total failure with little prospect of success.

2. Get to know the owner

You must spend time with the owner and in the business. Observation on its own will tell you a lot about the business, its level of management, its customer base and its reputation.

3. Initial meeting

Prepare well for your first meeting with the owner. Have a list of questions prepared about the business and discuss the price. The first meeting should provide you with sufficient information to decide whether or not to continue with negotiations.

4. Analyse the finances

You must have full access to the financial records of the company. You should have reputable auditors do what is called a due diligence examination of the business to see if it is what it claims to be. This examination will provide the basis for a realistic price for the business. You need to thoroughly check things such as:

- **Profit history:** This would include sales and profit as a percentage of sales. If there is a low return on your investment, you may be better off putting your money in the bank.
- **Debt levels:** This includes money owed to the bank and to suppliers.
- **Assets:** The assets range from money owed to the business through to any stock, plant, equipment or property. It is important that the values and condition are carefully checked.
- **Financial commitments:** You need to have a full list of all financial commitments, from wage agreements through to retirement fund and medical aid schemes; leases on property or equipment; and motor vehicle allowances.
- **Taxes:** You must ensure that the tax position of the company is sound and up to date (what is owed to the Receiver of Revenue and municipal rates).
- **Work in progress:** All business under way and revenue expected should be checked.

5. Check all agreements and documentation

All agreements and documentation must be checked, from labour agreements through to the documentation relating to the actual establishment of the business.

6. Measure the business against your business plan

Your own business plan for the acquisition will help you to identify problems and find the solutions.

7. Setting the price

Once the business has been properly assessed, you can negotiate the final price. There are a number of different ways in which you can base price, the most common being payback of capital. This calculation is based on how long it will take the business to generate the profit to pay back your investment within a set period. The most commonly accepted period is between two and three years.

8. Final documentation

Make sure that everything is properly documented. Do not accept verbal assurances. Everything must be confirmed in writing. Again, you should have everything checked by experts, particularly by your accountant and lawyer.

3. BUYING INTO AN EXISTING BUSINESS

There are significant advantages to buying into an existing business, or joining forces with others to start a new business. Advantages include:

- A pooling of resources, particularly financial resources, which can make an otherwise marginal business viable, among other things reducing the need for a high debt load.
- Complementary skills, which will always strengthen a business. For example, if a business has someone with technical skills and another with management skills, the chances of success are far greater.
- Spotting all the opportunities, which you cannot always do as a single player.

On top of all the issues listed in purchasing a business, when you buy into an existing business you must also consider and record in a contract the ownership structure and responsibilities of the joint owners.

4. A FRANCHISE

Setting up a business as part of a franchise is becoming an increasingly popular choice, both locally and internationally. A franchise means that you own your business, but you have to play by the rules of the franchiser. In some ways it is like buying into an existing business, but the financial risks are all yours.

There are many advantages to buying into a franchise. These include:

- You know before you start that the underlying business idea is sound.
- The franchiser will hold your hand through all aspects of the start-up.
- Established franchises have a strong brand identity (name recognition by consumers), and the franchiser continues to run promotion campaigns that reinforce the brand. The stronger the brand, the more you are likely to pay to become a franchisee.
- Most franchises provide input discounts because of the bulk buying of the entire franchise.
- In most cases you will have access to training, both for yourself and your staff.
- Most franchises provide central back-up specialist services covering issues such as tax, labour and legal issues.
- Other franchisees will pass on experience and ideas to fellow franchisees.
- The franchiser is often able to arrange finance, but even if this facility is not available it will generally be easier to arrange finance.

Do not believe that a franchise is a total business solution. There can be problems. These include:

- Loss of freedom: You own your own business but you have to take orders from the franchiser. The franchiser may set standards covering everything from service levels to quality controls, and even the appearance and geographical position of your franchise.
- You are dependent on the entire franchise operation being well managed. If the franchiser or other franchisees get sloppy, it can also impact on your business.
- You are at the mercy of the franchiser continuing as a going concern, providing you with promised support, particularly in backing up the branding.
- A franchise can cost a lot of money. Normally there is an upfront fee, but there are also ongoing royalties, profit participation and service fees that may be included.

REVISITING YOUR START-UP PLANS

Your business plan is not only there to establish whether you have a viable business concept and to establish your business, but it is also your guiding light into the future. Everything you do must be measured against your initial plans. You must test all aspects of your business plan against what you predicted: the sales, costs, profits, control of debts and, most of all, cash flows.

An essential part of revisiting your business plan is budgeting. Proper budgeting is an essential business practice. Budgeting is simply a way of planning and ensuring that you have a successful business. It is a step-by-step process that will keep you disciplined. Once you have drawn up your budget you should monitor it on a regular basis, particularly when you launch your business. You will have to make constant adjustments, and you may find that you will have to rethink some fundamentals. You need short- and long-term budgets. Long-term budgets are there to set objectives over time, such as business expansion. Short-term budgets are there to police your business.

SHORT-TERM BUDGETS

Short-term budgets are normally drawn up for a period of six months to a year ahead. The budget then has to be measured on a regular basis to see whether reality is matching your plans. You should measure your business against your budget at least once a month. Any change in what you budgeted will be your early warning indicator that sales are flagging, or that expenses may be starting to creep up. This allows you to take early action.

Short-term budgets are simply another way of listing your spending and income targets. You should have budget figures for:

- **Income:** This includes sales and income from any other source.
- **Expenditure (costs):** This includes salaries, input costs and debt repayment.
- **Debtors and creditors:** You need to know how much you expect to owe or be owed at any particular time.
- **Profits:** You need to anticipate how much profit you may or may not make. You need to budget for both gross profit (sales less cost of sales) as well as net profit (sales less all costs of running your business).

- **Stock:** You need to be sure of how much stock you must order and how much you hold at any time. If you are holding too much stock, it means you have less cash available.

Drawing up a budget is not simply a matter of drawing up a wish list. It must be based on realisable facts and opinions. A budget is a planning process. Your business plan will play a major part in providing the foundation stones for a successful budget. There are four elements to a budget. These are:

1. Commitment

You and your staff need to have 'ownership' of the budget. Everyone on your staff should be included in planning budgets and setting targets. If targets are reached, they can be rewarded with bonuses.

2. What budgets to set

You need to decide on what budgets to set. These can range from sales to how much you will spend on new equipment for the year.

3. Collect the data

You need as much information as possible to draw up an accurate budget. If your business has been going for a while the process is much easier, as you have the records of previous years. With a new business you will have to make a lot of assumptions.

4. Compile the budgets

SHORT-TERM
BUDGETS

1. Commitment
2. What budgets
to set
3. Collect the data
4. Compile the
budgets

Using the data you have collected and the opinion of others, you are now ready to draw up your budget. As with many other management functions, you will again find it best to use a computer program that will allow for easy adjustments. Your budget sheet should have three columns for each item: the budgeted amount; the actual amount; and the difference (called the variable). The difference is the indicator of what you are getting right or wrong.

9

Moving Out

Late teens and early **twenties** are times of great change, not least because that is when most people **leave** home to start up on their own. More often than not this is an event that **happens** in stages. The final **stage** often comes when you have **your own** washing machine and you **do not** have to go back home **every** Sunday evening in order to have clean clothes for **Monday**.

Some people, those with a bit more money than most, manage to move out and into an apartment of their own – total freedom. Others, with less money, have to share digs with friends, but often also with total strangers. Making the move is a big thing. There will be changes in your lifestyle, but there will also be a major impact on your finances – and even if your parents are, for example, paying for you to stay in private digs while you are studying at university or tech, your attitude to finance will have to change.

Finding a new place to stay is fairly difficult. Very few people find a dream home at first go. More often than not, because of budget limitations, your first home away from home will have damp walls, cockroaches in the bathroom and a view of Joe's Scrap Metal yard. The main thing is, it is yours.

When you move out, you have a number of options all dictated by the size of the bulge in your wallet. Be warned that the housing market is fraught with difficulties. Whole books are written about single aspects of having your own home, from renting to sectional title to freehold title. In this chapter only the main issues will be raised, with the focus on renting and sharing accommodation.

As a general warning, in order to protect yourself ensure that agreements made are always in writing. If someone gives you a verbal undertaking or promise, write them a letter confirming what they have said. In this way, if there are later disagreements, there can be no disputes.

RENTING

As with most things, if you follow a step-by-step strategy, you lessen the chances of picking up a lemon. Rented accommodation is where most of us start, either renting a property individually or with a group of friends. The steps are:

1. FINDING THE RIGHT PLACE

Rented accommodation comes in many different forms. Here are some of the choices:

Single room: Most often single rooms that are rented out are in family homes, where someone like you has left to go elsewhere. In many cases you will be expected to fit in as another member of the family. If you want your privacy, you need to find a room with a separate entrance, its own bathroom and rudimentary cooking facilities, such as a hot plate and fridge. In some cases you will also be offered one or two meals a day and other facilities, such as laundry. You are likely to be charged a monthly rent that will cover everything that you are offered and accept. This will include water and lights. If you want to use the telephone, you should expect to pay extra.

Granny flats: Many people today build separate granny flats on their properties. They may either be attached to the main house or free standing. With a granny flat you will have a lot more privacy with a better level of facilities than a single room. However, it is unlikely that you will be allowed to hold any noisy parties or have hordes of people on the property. You will be charged a monthly rental, which may or may not include water and lights. A telephone would be your responsibility. In most cases you should expect to feed yourself. Watch out for things like being allowed to have guests staying over with you.

Communal residences: Near many educational institutions you will often find houses that are owned by people who stay somewhere else. They will let out all the rooms in the house to students. You have no say in who else is staying in the house. You will most often have to share bathroom and kitchen facilities. Because you are with strangers and people with different habits, it is essential that you move into a house that has an organised structure with some general rules (like keeping the bathroom and kitchen clean), or else there can be a lot of friction. In most cases you will pay an all-in rent that will cover water and lights, but you will have to feed yourself.

Private hotels and boarding houses: These are normally large old houses run by the owner, who usually also stays on the property. You will normally get a room with or without its own bathroom. You may have a choice of meals, for example only breakfast, or breakfast and dinner. The rental is likely to include water and lights. You will normally find that a telephone call box is available.

Shared accommodation: If you are responding to an advertisement to share accommodation, the person doing the advertising will either own the property or will be renting it from someone else. You will probably be expected to sign some type of agreement. You are likely to be allocated a room, again with or without a bathroom. You will have rights to the common areas of the house, such as the lounge, dining room and kitchen. You will pay rent and will probably also be expected to share in the costs of water and electricity.

Apartments and houses: Here you are moving into the area of more formal and legal arrangements. If you rent an apartment or house, you will be expected to sign a lease agreement (the conditions under which you will rent the house). Among other things, the lease agreement will state what you must pay in rent; by when it must be paid; if and when the rent can be increased; how many people may stay on the property; and even whether you will be permitted to keep pets. The lease agreement is mainly there to protect the owner of the property: to ensure that the rent is paid on time, and that when you leave the property it is in the same condition as when you received it.

A lease agreement also protects you. It will contain provisions for your privacy and your right to the use of the property. If you intend to share the accommodation, you must make sure that this is included in the agreement, as well as your right to collect rent from the other people sharing the accommodation.

It is best to have someone who is knowledgeable about leases, such as a lawyer, have a look at it to ensure you are properly protected.

2. HOW TO FIND A NEW HOME

- **Varsity and tech:** Many universities and technical colleges have lists of places that can be rented. These could vary from a single room to a house shared with others.
- **Supermarket notice boards:** Often places to rent or offers to share accommodation are placed on these boards. You can also put up your own notice stating that you are looking for a place, and the type of accommodation you are after.
- **Newspapers:** All newspapers publicise accommodation in their classified columns: apartments, granny flats, single rooms, houses for rent, etc. You will also find advertisements of people looking for others with whom to share accommodation. You can also place your own advertisement describing what you want.
- **Estate and letting agents:** If you know the area where you want to live, call in at estate agent offices in the vicinity. They will often have places for rent on their books, but these will mainly be apartments and houses.

3. RECORDING THE FACTS

There are a number of issues that must be decided and/or you should consider before you move in. These issues include:

Amenities: A wide range of amenities and other facilities should be considered, for example, off-street parking; if there is a pool, can you use it; laundry facilities; and television aerials.

Deposits: In most cases you will be required to put down a refundable deposit equal to at least one month's rent. This is to ensure that the person leasing the property will not suffer any loss if you suddenly decide to leave, or you do serious damage to the property. In the lease agreement it should be recorded that you will receive interest at a particular rate on your deposit, and how and when the deposit will be repaid to you.

Furnishings: Is the apartment furnished, partly furnished or unfurnished? There are advantages and disadvantages to both. Furnished accommodation tends to be more expensive, but then you also do not have the upfront cost of buying furniture, stoves and fridges. In apartments and houses the stove is normally installed.

Lease (rental) agreement: Is the accommodation/apartment available on a month-to-month basis, or is there a formal lease agreement? Many rental agreements are for one year. At a minimum, you are required to give one month's notice of breaking off a lease agreement. A one-month notice requirement may also apply when you are staying in a private house or a boarding house. You should have a clause written into the lease agreement that states that, should you have to move out due to unforeseen circumstances, you should be allowed to find a suitable person to replace you. Do not sign any agreement that you have not read and properly understood. If you are in any doubt consult another party, such as a lawyer.

Maintenance: Who is responsible for the proper maintenance of the property? This can differ from agreement to agreement, with you being responsible for some things and your landlord or lady being responsible for others.

Other tenants: If you are sharing accommodation, take the time to meet the other tenants to see if you can get on.

Security: Unfortunately, it is increasingly important to take security into account. For example, is there a security system such as security guards or alarms? An insurance company will charge you premiums for your personal effects according to the level of security on the property.

Rent or board: Most often the monthly rental is due in advance. Most people want their money by the first of the month, but will often give you a few days leeway. Increasingly, in private digs for students you are expected to pay rent six months or even a year in advance. It is often best to pay the rent by way of a stop order on your bank account to ensure that it is paid on time. As a general guide it is best to keep rent to below 25 percent of your gross income. If you go above this level it could seriously disrupt your budget, and your life could become a total drag with no money for anything.

Utilities: Additional charges for water, lights and rates can all vary, from paying nothing, to paying a set amount, to paying a share. If you are responsible for the utilities, you may also find you have to get yourself connected. This will involve paying a deposit to the local municipality.

4. WHEN YOU MOVE IN

When you move in you should check everything thoroughly for your own protection. For example, ensure that all plug points work, taps work, drains are not blocked, and that the condition of carpets and walls is good. If there are any problems, notify the agent or owner immediately in writing (not merely verbally). If you want to put a new coat of paint on a wall, check that this is acceptable to the owner.

SHARING WITH OTHERS

The first step to moving out of your family home is normally to move in with others. You need to be very careful on two points. The first is selecting your housemates; and the second is setting the rules and boundaries for living together. The second applies even more where you have had no choice in your housemates.

In choosing housemates, you need to first draw up a comprehensive list of questions, to see whether you have the same general interests. For example, if you are religious, a non-smoker and do not drink, enjoy classical music and prefer a quiet life, you may find it difficult living with someone whose idea of life is to get drunk every Friday night, play techno music all day and go to raves at night (or vice versa). Here are the steps you should follow:

Step One: A written list of questions. The questions should include full personal details: name, age, educational qualifications, interests, hobbies, broad political views, religious inclinations, employment and approximate income (the last to make sure that they can pay the rent). Questions should also be asked about personal habits such as drinking, smoking, level of tidiness, attitude to drugs, tolerance for noise and the ability to make noise, pet peeves, sleeping hours, cooking abilities and eating habits (vegetarian or carnivore).

Step Two: The interview. You should have at least two interviews. One would be a straightforward affair where you would ask all the questions on the list. If you and your other housemates agree that the person is a candidate, then you should have a second interview, preferably in relaxed circumstances (e.g. supper or lunch) at which you can get to know the person a bit better and find out whether they have any habits that would drive you crazy. Incidentally, if you are the subject of an interview, do not pretend to be something you are not. It could make your life more difficult later.

Step Three: The agreement. It is essential that you and your housemates have a written agreement signed by everyone. The agreement must list things such as the rent, deposit and any other payments; when the payments are due; use and sharing of any facilities; how and who provides household supplies (this can be both food and/or cleaning materials); cleaning responsibilities; cooking responsibilities; a policy on having guests to stay; what is not permitted, like drugs and/or smoking; parties; study time; and finally, the most important, conflict resolution. You will have to decide what mechanism you will use to resolve conflicts. For example, you could bring in an outsider, such as the property owner; or you could opt for majority vote. If you have had no choice in your housemates, you must get together and draw up a similar agreement.

OWNING YOUR OWN HOME

There are two main ways in which South Africans can purchase residential property. These are sectional title and freehold title:

Freehold title: Freehold title gives you total and sole ownership of your property. You make all the decisions and are responsible for all upkeep. Freehold title is a form of ownership that applies mainly to free-standing houses. You can have sectional title ownership of a free-standing house where there is common ownership of the land.

Sectional title: Sectional title ownership applies mainly to blocks of apartments where there is common property, such as common walls and a garden. What this means is that you own your portion (or section) of the property that you occupy, and share common parts of the property with all your co-owners. You and your co-owners form a committee, called a body corporate, which decides how the property should be managed. You need to pay a levy for the maintenance of the common property, and maybe even for such things as security services.

Sectional title holds many more potential pitfalls for owners than freehold title. Issues you must consider with sectional title include:

- Details of areas of common ownership.
- What common rules apply to the property, such as are animals allowed, parking, noise at night?
- Who are the property managers, what are their duties and how much are they paid?
- The monthly levy and what the levy covers.
- Whether the body corporate has any debts. If it has debts you will be taking on a proportional share of the debt load. (The body corporate is elected by all the owners to manage the property, including making rules.)
- Whether the body corporate has any assets. Likewise, you then own a share of the assets.
- Are any major renovations planned in the next year or so? Would this involve you in extra cost?
- What is the general condition of the building and property?
- The members of the body corporate. Meet them. They may not be very pleasant people or have very different views from yourself about how the common property should be maintained.
- What conflict resolution mechanisms exist in the event of a dispute?

WHAT TO CONSIDER WHEN BUYING PROPERTY

When buying property, whether by sectional or freehold title, you are making one of the bigger investments of your life. You need to approach property ownership very carefully and must take a number of issues into account. You should also look at a variety of properties so that you can get an idea of prices for areas and the condition of different properties. There are six steps, most of which entail a number of subsidiary issues that you must take into account when buying property. These are:

1. ASSESSING THE PROPERTY

You need to make a proper assessment of whether the property is suitable for you before you make an offer to purchase. There are seven issues you need to assess. These are:

1. Pressure selling

Do not be pressurised into buying. The most common pressure is for the agent to tell you that there are six other buyers waiting around the corner. If you miss a purchase there will always be another.

2. Position

The biggest issue in buying property is position, position and position. The position of the property is important because that will determine how easily you will be able to resell. Facts you need to consider in buying in the right place are crime levels, proximity to shops, schools and other amenities, noise levels (for example, is it next to a motorway), general popularity of the area and the condition of nearby properties.

3. Accurate pricing

Ask the estate agent for a list of selling prices of other properties in the area to give you a guide. Also visit show houses in the area to see what you can expect to pay for similar properties. Do not agree to the asking price. Negotiate.

4. Affordability

There are two main issues you need to take into account in deciding whether you can afford the purchase. These are price and additional costs:

Price

You cannot really afford the property if:

- You cannot put down 20 percent of the price as a deposit. (If you borrow more than 80 percent of the value of the property, the banks are obliged by the Reserve Bank to charge you penalty interest rates

on the additional 20 percent); and/or
- If you need to pay more than 25 percent of your after-tax income to repay the loan.

You should also take into account what will happen if interest rates go up. In 1998, when interest rates skyrocketed to 25 percentage points, many people lost their homes because they could no longer afford the repayments. This is something you must consider when interest rates are low.

Costs

Initial costs can add considerably to the purchase price of a home. These costs include:

- Transfer taxes. Transfer taxes are based on the purchase price (normally, but not always if the South African Revenue Service considers that you have paid too little). From March 2002 there is no transfer tax up to R100 000; between R100 001 and R300 000 there is 5 percent on the value above R100 000; and 8 percent on any amount above R300 001.
- Bond registration agreements, which are upwards of R2 000.
- Lawyers' fees (upwards of R500).
- Bank valuation fees (R1 000 plus).
- Electricity and water connection deposits.
- Moving costs.

Annual costs include:

- Rates. These can be high if you are in an upmarket area. (Incidentally, ensure that rates, water and electricity bills are paid up to date, or you may find yourself responsible for any backlog.)
- Maintenance. As a rough estimate, you can expect maintenance costs of at least R500 a month for a modest, three-bedroom home.
- Water and lights.

5. Condition

If the property is in a poor condition, you may be involved in significant additional expenses. You must insist on receiving a list of all faults in writing. If a fault is hidden from you at sale you have the right to rescind the sale. If you are in any doubt about the condition of the property, get an expert in to inspect it.

6. Neighbourhood

There are two things you need to assess in the neighbourhood:

- Get the feel of the area. Often estate agents will drive you to the property on a route selected for its attractiveness, while a block away there may be an industrial area.
- Meet the people living next to you. If the neighbours are crotchety, you may have to live with endless complaints.

7. Building regulations

You need to check whether there are any special building restrictions that could limit renovations or alterations that you may want to make in the future.

2. HOW TO OWN THE PROPERTY

There are a number of ways in which you can own a property, from it being in your own name through to it being owned in a trust, a close corporation or a company. The issues you need to consider include:

- Your personal circumstances. For example, if you and/or a spouse are involved in a business partnership that leaves your personal assets vulnerable to creditors if something goes wrong in the business, you should consider placing the property in a trust; and
- Capital gains tax: You will not get the R1 million exemption from CGT if the property is not owned by an individual (i.e. it is owned in a trust or company structure).

3. SIGNING AN OFFER TO PURCHASE

Most offers to purchase are fairly standard, but you do not have to accept all the clauses and there is nothing to prevent you from adding other conditions. Any offer to purchase must be in the name of the entity in which you want to own the property, for example your name, or that of a trust or company.

Your offer to purchase must include all conditions, such as:

- A description of the property.
- The offer price.
- The size of the deposit and how it will be paid. Insist that the deposit is held in a money market account with the interest accruing to you. If you do not ask you may not get the interest.
- How and when the full purchase price will be paid.
- The conditions of occupation. You must be particularly careful of occupational interest that you may have to pay before you take transfer. You must negotiate a set figure that would be equivalent to rentals in the area. A normal rate is one percent of purchase price.
- When the property will be transferred into your name.
- What fittings will be included (you must list these).
- The financing of the purchase. If you are raising a home loan, the purchase is normally made dependent on your being able to raise the money from a bank.
- Other conditions of purchase, such as it being dependent on the successful sale of another property you may own.
- What repairs or maintenance needs to be done by the current owner.
- The provision by the seller of electrical and beetle certificates.
- Guarantees and undertakings on the condition of the property and the purchase agreement. Remember that most homes are bought 'voetstoots', which means in their existing condition. You only have a comeback if the seller has deliberately hidden or misled you about a problem.
- Brokerage paid to the estate agent. Although the seller pays this, the amount can often determine the outcome of the purchase. Estate agents, despite the fact that inflation works in their favour, have managed to ratchet up commission levels to 7.5 percent of the purchase price, plus VAT. This totals 8.55 percent, which is ridiculous. If this commission is negotiated down to about 5 percent, which is still more than generous, it can affect the price you will pay. Remember, commissions on lump-sum investments are normally about 3 percent, so why estate agents should receive so much more is debatable.

4. RAISING THE FINANCE

The financing of your property is extremely important. There are five issues you need to take into account. These are:

1. Arrange your own home loan (mortgage bond)

Don't let the estate agent do it for you. You can often negotiate lower rates of interest with a bank by arranging your own home loan. Estate agents get paid a reward by a bank for bringing in your home loan, and that fee will be included in what you pay in interest. There are people, called mortgage originators, who will negotiate loans on your behalf, but remember that you are also indirectly paying them.

2. Negotiate

Establish the current prime interest rate, then approach all the banks and other home loan financiers, such as SA Homeloans, which recently introduced a new form of 'securitised' home loans. (SA Homeloans borrows money from institutions to lend money at cheap rates. Its entry into the market made home loans a lot more competitive.) Even half a percent difference in interest rates will make a substantial difference to how much you will pay over the life of a bond. This is one significant area where a good credit rating will work in your favour.

3. Type of loan

Home loans are made available in a number of ways. These include:

- Traditional home loans: Home loans normally cover a period of 20 years, which you can pay off over the period. If you need more money, say for alterations, you have to apply for a re-advance. A re-advance takes time and will involve additional expenses, such as valuation fees.
- Variable amount bonds: These bonds come under various names, but are mainly known as access bonds. They allow you to increase or decrease the loan amount at your discretion. While this is a useful facility, variable bonds are often misused, with people drawing money for consumption expenditure, such as living expenses, and, even worse, for things such as holidays. You are undermining your asset base if you constantly use a variable bond to fund your day-to-day expenses. It means you are living beyond your means.

- Consolidated debt loans: Increasingly, banks are offering single-debt facilities, which include your home loan and other financing deals, such as motor vehicles. Initially these facilities were only for the wealthy. You had to earn more than R500 000 a year and own assets worth a few million. Now banks are starting to offer these facilities to ordinary customers in good standing.

4. Interest rate structure

Home loan borrowers are being given increasing choices in interest rate structures. These include:

- Variable rate loans: This is the most common interest rate structure for home loans. Your interest rate will move in parallel with what is called the prime overdraft lending rate. So, if you have a rate of one percent below prime, it will remain one percent below when the prime rate goes up or down;
- Fixed rates: Most banks will offer fixed rates for periods of up to 18 or 24 months. The fixed rates tend to be higher than variable rates at the date when you fix the rate. However, you do have certainty of what rate you will be paying, particularly at times of interest rate volatility. Anyone who borrowed on a fixed rate in July 1998, when interest rates were around 14 percent, was laughing when by August rates were nudging up to 25 percent. Fixed rates come with various bells and whistles, such as reductions if rates do fall by a certain amount.

5. Insurance

A bank will insist on numerous conditions, such as your having life assurance to cover repayment of the loan in case you die, or are disabled and unable to earn an income; and short-term insurance to ensure that if there is significant damage to the property, you can afford the repair costs. The bond issuer can decide which short-term insurance company must be used to provide the insurance on your home (normally no one can dictate which company should be used), while you decide on the life assurer.

5. TAKING TRANSFER

Once the seller has accepted your option to purchase and the bank has provided finance (if required), the lawyers take over. The lawyers register the property in your name; the mortgage bond is registered; you pay the transfer tax; and the seller is paid out. A Deed of Sale is issued showing that you now own the property. If you have a mortgage bond, the bank retains the papers as part of its security.

6. MAKING IT TRULY YOURS

Many people consider a house to be theirs, no matter how large the debt. It is not. Your home effectively belongs to the bank until you have paid off your home loan. Most housing mortgage bonds are for 20 years. However, if you pay off the bond earlier, you will save yourself a lot of money.

Let's take a mortgage bond for R200 000 as an example: you are paying interest at a nominal rate of 14 percent a year. The minimum monthly repayment to pay off the bond over 20 years is R2 487.04. This means that over 20 years you will repay R596 889.60 – almost three times what you borrowed.

However, if you increase your repayments by only R100 a month, you will repay the bond in 16 years and eight months, and save yourself R78 964.

If you increase your repayments by R500 a month, you will repay the bond in 10 years and 10 months and save yourself R205 617.

The quicker you pay off the bond, the more you will save in interest charges and the sooner your home will be truly yours.

10

Getting Wheels

The dream of every teenager is to get wheels. Motorised transport brings freedom. That is, freedom to come and go as you please. But be warned: wheels can also curtail your freedom as surely as having your feet nailed to the ground.

Most of us think only of the price of the car. We scour newspaper advertisements, look at the different types of cars and their prices and spend hours discussing makes, models, colours and engines. Very seldom does anyone discuss what it costs to keep a car on the road – that is the really expensive part. You must not only consider the initial cost, but all the other costs. These include: insurance, petrol and oil, servicing, annual licensing and repairs. Do you know that a major service can cost more than R1 000? The cheaper and older the car, the higher the repair bills are likely to be.

The biggest mistakes people make in buying motor vehicles are:

- They buy the biggest and the best, which is often out of their price range, saddling themselves with high debt.
- They buy new motor vehicles when they could make a considerable saving by buying a good, second-hand, recent model.
- They replace motor vehicles too quickly. Most cars will last you at least eight years, if not longer, depending on the mileage you do. If you keep replacing a car every three years you are adding to your costs, as a

new vehicle loses at least 20 percent of its value as you drive out the showroom door.

- They choose an inappropriate form of borrowing, with high interest rates and other add-on costs.
- They buy vehicles that have high running and servicing costs, guzzle petrol and need expensive spare parts.
- They forget that the more costly or sporty a vehicle, the higher the premium they will pay in insurance.
- They add on fancy parts, which are excessively expensive.

How to go about buying a car

There are 10 steps to follow when buying a motor vehicle. These are:

1. HOW MUCH SHOULD YOU SPEND?

Work out how much money you have. This will give you a starting point for the type of vehicle you can afford. If you are under 21, the banks will not allow you to borrow money without support and agreement from your parents. Cars are what are called depreciating assets (they lose value the older they get), so you should avoid borrowing money to buy one. Interest on car financing is quite high as well. You are also unlikely to be able to borrow money from a motor vehicle financing bank to buy a car that is more than four or five years old.

2. FINANCING

If you are unable to pay cash or get bank finance, you may need to borrow money from relatives. The cheapest way would probably be to ask your parents to increase their home loan and charge you the interest rate they would have to pay. Other ways to finance the purchase of a motor vehicle include hire purchase and lease agreements.

Hire purchase agreement

HP agreements, as hire purchase agreements are generally called, are loans that are mainly made available through banks, but increasingly by divisions of motor vehicle manufacturers and larger motor vehicle retailers. The elements of HP agreements are:

- You are leasing (hiring) the vehicle until you have repaid the loan – then, and only then, does the vehicle become yours.
- If you default on the loan the financier of the deal is entitled to reclaim the vehicle, and you can lose everything you have paid.
- You need a deposit of at least 20 percent.
- The repayment period is a maximum of 54 months.
- The interest rates tend to be higher than for a home loan; in some cases they are excessive. You need to negotiate the rate.
- There are likely to be additional administration charges.
- You will not find it easy to negotiate the price of a motor vehicle, as you are not paying cash.
- The terms and conditions of a loan can be onerous. You need to check the terms carefully. One of the most important issues is repayment. Some lenders make it difficult to repay the loan quicker, with penalties for early repayment.

Lease

Lease arrangements are different from a hire purchase agreement in that you are in effect only hiring the vehicle, unlike an HP agreement, which entails leasing and purchase. Here are the main elements of this type of financing:

- Lease arrangements are suitable for businesses and for people with motor vehicle allowances, because you can claim the cost of the lease proportionally against business mileage.
- No deposit is required.
- The maximum lease period is five years.
- In most cases you effectively pay interest on the sale price of the vehicle at a higher than normal interest rate.
- You can take ownership of the vehicle when the lease period expires. The amount you pay will depend on the structure of the lease. Many of these deals have residual or balloon payments at the end. Residual value financing allows you to buy a vehicle that you would not normally be able to afford.

A residual payment is structured like this:
- You pay a monthly lease, which is lower than a hire purchase instalment.
- You leave an unpaid large sum, called a residual or balloon payment, until the end of the contract period. The average residual value over

five years is anything between 20 percent and 35 percent of the new cost of the vehicle.

- In theory, the residual payment should be equal to the resale value. So, when the contract expires you should be able to sell the car for its residual value and owe nothing.

There are two major disadvantages of taking out a residual value contract, namely higher cost and the possibility of receiving a lower than expected residual value:

Problem 1: Higher cost

Over time, it costs you more to enter into a residual contract than a straight instalment sale contract. For example, a R200 000 vehicle at an interest rate of 15.5 percent over 60 months would cost you almost R14 000 more with residual value financing than it would with conventional financing.

The interest on a standard instalment contract would be R84 958. The same car on similar terms would cost you interest of R98 600 in terms of a residual value contract with payment on 20 percent of the value of the car deferred. But ultimately you would pay R138 600 (R98 600 interest plus the R40 000, which is the 20 percent residual) that was deferred.

Problem 2: Lower than expected value

There is a risk of the market value of the vehicle being less than the residual value at the end of the contract. In many cases it is impossible to settle the contract early, because there is very little capital repayment in the initial period of the agreement. You need to know from the outset how much the residual amount is going to be, and that you will not be relying on the sale of the vehicle to pay off the residual.

Making use of a residual makes ownership more affordable initially, and you might rationalise that your income will be much higher in four or five years when the residual payment falls due. At that time, if you do not have the cash, you might be able to refinance the vehicle for the residual amount. Some banks will check the condition of your vehicle to make sure that its current value is more or less equivalent to the amount that you still owe.

As a general guide, any residual over 40 percent of the initial purchase price could be too high and should be carefully checked out. A rule of thumb when deciding on the size of the residual that is appropriate for you is to expect your vehicle to depreciate by one percent a month for the duration of your contract. So, if your contract term is 60 months, your car will depreciate by 60 percent over the period. This means that you should not have a greater than 40 percent residual.

To avoid owing the bank more than you could get by selling the car, you could opt for a buy-back contract with a motor dealer, who guarantees to buy back your vehicle for a certain value after a set time, provided you have not done more than a specified number of kilometres.

Other issues to take into account with residual financing include:

- **Abuses:** There are some serious abuses of the residual system. Some franchise dealers, who sell cars that do not retain their value well, approach a bank offering to place all their business with that bank in return for financing at least a 40 percent residual on every deal. These dealerships then advertise cars with super-low repayments, such as 'only R999 a month'. While it is a contravention of the Advertising Standards Authority's Code of Conduct not to disclose the residual amount, very often the information is buried in the fine print.
- **Residual amount:** The size of the residual that the bank will allow you will depend on the risk you pose to the bank. Ideally, the size of the residual should be linked to the expected trade-in value of the vehicle, but banks may apply stricter or easier credit criteria to residual value financing because of the buyer's responsibility to make good any short-fall between the value of the vehicle and the residual value.
- **Final value of the vehicle:** The actual residual value of the vehicle will to a large extent be determined by the condition of the vehicle and the distance covered. Poor condition and a high kilometre reading on the odometer will result in a lower market value when you choose to sell it. As much as 20 percent can be deducted from the book value if the vehicle is in a poor condition with many kilometres on the clock. Then you could find your car worth only 25 percent of what you owe the bank to settle the residual.

    If you are likely to run up a high mileage, you should investigate the maintenance contracts offered by some motor dealers.
- **Insurance:** You must make sure that the insurance covers the entire value of your motor vehicle, including the residual payment. If your insurance policy does not cover the outstanding balance of your loan and you have an accident in which the vehicle is written off, you could find yourself carrying a heavy financial burden.

3. NEW OR SECOND HAND

Depending on how much money you have, you can decide whether you can afford a new car or whether you are confined to the second-hand market. There is nothing wrong with owning a second-hand car. You can get some very good bargains – but again, be warned, as you can get some absolute lemons, which come with only one guarantee: it will last as long as it takes the salesperson to bank your money.

If you have enough money to buy a new car, rather consider buying a demonstration model (these are new cars used to give demonstration drives to buyers) or a car from a car-hire firm. These cars have normally done very few kilometres and are usually in very good condition, but are quite a bit cheaper than a new car.

4. CHOOSING A NEW CAR

If you have enough money to buy a new car, decide on your price limit and look at the motoring supplements published every week in the newspapers. The supplements list the new cars available and their prices. Once you have narrowed down your choice, test-drive your selection. Don't pay the first price you are given. As you are probably paying cash, you can get the price reduced. Visit all the franchise dealers in your town that are selling the make and model you want, and establish their prices. You could save yourself a few thousand rand.

> If you are buying a new car, advance to Step Eight.
> If you are buying a second-hand car, advance to Step Five.

5. FINDING A SECOND-HAND CAR

Try to find someone who knows someone in the car industry. There is a book called the *Auto Dealer's Digest*, which places prices on all second-hand cars. There is an upper price at which the second-hand car dealers normally sell a second-hand car, and a lower price at which they buy them. With this book you would get a very good idea of prices.

You can either buy second-hand cars privately from someone else, or through a second-hand dealer. You will probably get a better price in a private sale, but a sale through a dealer can come with some guarantees on the motor vehicle itself. When buying from a dealer, make sure that you are dealing with a registered member of the Retail Motor Industry, as you will have some comeback if anything goes very wrong. There is a Motor Industry Adjudicator to whom you can take complaints. The e-mail address is: mi.ombudsman@netactive.co.za.

Private owners and second-hand dealers advertise cars and motorbikes every day in the classified sections of your local newspaper. Take your time buying a second-hand car. Look around, spend your time test-driving vehicles – don't be pressurised into making a quick buy (there are literally thousands of second-hand cars for sale).

6. FINAL CHECKS

Before making an offer to buy a second-hand car, either in a private sale or through a dealer, here are a few tips to protect you from buying something that will pack up around the first corner:

- Don't pay anything – a deposit or anything else – until you are satisfied with the purchase you are making.
- Check the service record book to ensure that it has been serviced regularly.
- Take it to the Automobile Association (AA). For a fee, the AA will give the car a thorough going-over. In a private sale, get the owner to pay half the fee, because if you decide not to buy the car they will know exactly what is wrong with it, and will be able to get it fixed, making a sale to someone else much easier. If there is no branch of the AA near you, take the car to the garage your family uses to have it checked.
- Insist that the current owner put the car through a roadworthiness check. You cannot get the car licensed in your name unless it has a Certificate of Roadworthiness (CoR). This will give you additional peace of mind. Most second-hand car dealers provide a CoR in the price automatically, but this is not a guarantee of condition as bribes are often paid for CoR certificates.
- When test-driving a car or motorbike, don't only drive around the block. Take it out on the motorway and see what happens at speed. Also, take in a few hills and keep going for about half an hour, so that you can see if any odd noises develop or the engine starts overheating. Test the brakes and ensure that the vehicle does not pull in any particular direction when you brake.
- Check the engine. Give-away signs of poor condition include puffs of smoke from the exhaust when the car starts or when you change gear; a

rough feeling to the gears; a grey colour to the oil, which means seals are inefficient and water is mixing with the oil; any jerkiness when the motor is running. Wait a while after parking the car, then check under it for oil and water leaks.

- Check the odometer. The lower the odometer reading, the better. An easy indication is that you can expect a distance of about 20 000 km a year. Anything less is an indication that someone may have tampered with the odometer. When you have the car checked by the AA, ask them to check whether the odometer has been altered.

- Check the body for rust and previous collisions. Give-aways are slightly different colours on different parts and body filler (use a magnet on the body – where it does not stick is a sure sign of body filler). Rust shows up on window edges (look under the rubber), behind boot and door panels and at joints.

- Check that you are not buying a 'Code 3' vehicle. This is the classification given by traffic departments to vehicles that have been scrapped and rebuilt.

7. STOLEN VEHICLES

There are many stolen cars on the road in South Africa. If you buy a stolen car and it is tracked to you, the police will take it away and you will lose your money. For this reason you must be particularly careful when you buy a second-hand car. Here are a few tips:

- In a private sale, ensure that the name and address of the registered owner tally with the identification book of the seller. (Ask to see identification.)

- Check the engine and chassis numbers on the vehicle against the registration documents.

- If you are in any doubt, check with the police or your local traffic department. They have access to the National Traffic Information System (Natis), an online database that records ownership details of all registered vehicles on our roads. You can also telephone AA Autocheck on 0861 601 601. You will need the vehicle's chassis number, engine number, make, model, year, mileage and colour.

- If you are buying from a private buyer or a small second-hand operation, ensure that no money is owed on the car. Enquire about previous owners and how they financed the purchase. Check with the institution that financed the loan that it has been paid off. If the car is being leased and there is still a financing agreement in place, you will have problems, as the car was not the seller's to sell.

- Never pay for any vehicle in cash. Either pay with a bank-guaranteed cheque or a personal cheque, with the cheque made out to the seller and endorsed as 'not transferable'.

8. LICENSING, REGISTRATION AND NUMBER PLATES

If you are buying a new car from a dealer or dealing with a reputable second-hand car dealer, they will arrange these things for you. You will have to pay the cost. If you are buying the car from a private buyer or a small second-hand operation, get the car registered in your name as quickly as possible. You can get the necessary papers, which must be signed by the current owner and yourself, from the motor vehicle licensing department in your town. You will need the signed documents and the CoR to get the car registered in your name.

9. GUARANTEES AND MAINTENANCE CONTRACTS

Carefully check what is guaranteed and what is not. For example, is labour guaranteed? The terms of guarantee are particularly important on used cars. On new cars they tend to be fairly similar.

Motor vehicle dealers sell maintenance contracts to cover the ongoing costs of maintaining your vehicle. The contracts do cost, but they ensure that you stick to the proper service intervals. Costs vary according to what the maintenance contract covers. Some include service costs, others include minor faults and others even include free tyre replacement after two years. The end result is that the car could be in a more marketable condition when you trade it in or sell it.

10. INSURANCE

It is important that you have the car insured before you drive it out of the garage. You could have an accident on the first bend ... and then it is all over. You can get three types of insurance:

- **Comprehensive insurance:** With this type of insurance your car is covered against anyone your car hits, any other vehicle your car hits or anything else your car hits. As the name implies, your car is comprehensively insured. If you have a new car or a moderately new second-hand car, you should get this type of insurance.

- **Third party, fire and theft:** This type of insurance is really there for older second-hand cars. Your car is only insured if it is stolen or catches fire. However, if you are involved in an accident and you damage someone else's property or injure someone else, you are covered.
- **Third party motor vehicle assurance:** This is compulsory assurance that you pay without even knowing it every time you buy petrol. This assurance covers anyone injured in an accident.

In deciding whether to take out comprehensive insurance you should not be asking yourself a question about the age of the car, but rather what would happen if your car is written off. Could you afford to replace it or not? If you cannot afford to replace it, then you should consider comprehensive insurance.

As you are under the age of 25, you will pay high insurance premiums. You will also have to pay a higher than normal excess if you have an accident. The word 'excess' is used to describe the first part that everyone must pay if they have an accident. So, say someone aged 26 had an accident that cost R10 000, he or she may have to pay the first R1 000. But if the driver was 21, they may have to pay an initial excess of the first R2 000. The reason for this is that accident records show that young people have more accidents than older drivers.

Here are four tips on car insurance:

- Never let a car dealer arrange your insurance. He will get a big commission and will not shop around for the cheapest rate. You should get hold of a broker or your bank and ask them to get you a list of quotations.
- Make sure that every year when you renew your insurance the value of the car is brought down. This is the biggest insurance racket going. You keep being charged a premium based on the original value, but if you wreck your car you will only be paid the current value.
- You can negotiate the excess you must pay. If you choose to pay a higher excess, then the cost of your insurance will come down. In deciding on an excess, take into account what you can afford to pay yourself. There is no point in having an excess of R5 000 if you cannot afford it.
- If you do not make an insurance claim in any year, you will build up a no-claim bonus, which reduces your insurance premiums. So, if you have

a small accident and the costs involved are, say, R2 300, and your excess is R2 000, it may be worth your paying the whole R2 300 and not losing your no-claim bonus.

When you have bought the car

Once you have bought your first car the real responsibility begins. By law you cannot have a car on the road that is not in good working order. Apart from possibly breaking the law, you should also ensure that your car is in good condition for your own safety and that of your passengers. It will need to be serviced regularly, and you should also check that lights, brake lights, etc. are always in good working condition. If your car is not in a sound condition, an insurance company can (and often will) refuse to pay a claim.

11

Protecting What You Own

When you start owning more and more valuable items, it is time to consider protecting your assets (what you own). When it comes to protecting your assets, you must include yourself.

Before you go any further in this chapter, read this carefully: insurance in all its forms is necessary. Unfortunately there are a fair number of very unscrupulous people in this industry, and they make a special effort to target young people, who they believe they can pressure into buying unnecessary insurance. The reason why unscrupulous people are attracted to this industry is because of the high commissions that are paid to people who sell insurance. Many people selling insurance products are only interested in the commission they are earning, and not in your financial well-being. You are seen as the sucker. Having said this, there are very good people working in the industry who will put your interests first. The problem is identifying the good ones from the bad ones. There are some guidelines later in this chapter on choosing the right person.

This chapter will divide into five parts: short-term insurance, life assurance (long-term insurance), estate planning (what happens when you die), medical assurance and how to choose a financial adviser.

SHORT-TERM INSURANCE

Insurance is normally the term used to cover the loss of or damage to things you own (short-term insurance), as well as death or disablement (long-term assurance). Short-term insurance is normally renewable every year, whereas long-term assurance is a long-term contract.

You take out short-term insurance to ensure that if your possessions are irreparably damaged through no fault of your own (this does not include normal wear and tear), or are stolen or lost, you will not suddenly have to find the money to replace them. You are taking a bet against a short-term insurance company on whether your assets (what you own) will suffer some misfortune. In return for paying a monthly or yearly amount, the insurance company will replace your goods or pay you out if you suffer a misfortune.

SHORT-TERM INSURANCE CAN BE EXPENSIVE

Short-term insurance costs (premiums) can be very expensive. The premiums you pay will depend on a number of factors. These include:

- **Your age:** This is particularly the case for a motor vehicle, because younger people have far more accidents than older people.
- **Where you live:** If you live in a high crime area, you will pay more for your insurance.
- **Level of security:** If your home has a good alarm system, you will pay less.
- **Level of insurance:** You can choose between being paid out at the new replacement cost, or at the cost you paid for the item, or at the current value of the item.
- **History of claims:** If you claim often, you will pay higher premiums.
- **Age of the items:** You will pay less for insurance on a used car than a new model because it is worth less.
- **Cost of item:** The more expensive the item, the more you pay in premiums.

HOW TO REDUCE INSURANCE COSTS

There are a number of ways to reduce the costs of short-term insurance. These include:

Excess: Whenever you take out short-term insurance, you will always find a reference to excess. This means that whenever you claim, you will have to pay the first so many hundred or thousand rand of any claim. For example, say you crash your car and the cost of repairs is R2 000, you may be asked to pay the first R500 or R1 000, with the insurance company paying the rest. The reason for this is to stop people claiming for every little thing. Imagine how much administration the insurance company would have to do if every time you lost or broke a coffee mug you made a claim. It would make insurance impossibly expensive. Sometimes the insurance company places an additional excess on your insurance. One of the most regular examples is for drivers under the age of 25, because young drivers have far more accidents. But you can also place a voluntary excess on your insurance. Say the excess you have to pay is R1 000, and you make it R3 000, the cost of your premiums will be lower. However, you must be sure that you can cover the cost of the excess. In other words, if you crash your car and you have to pay an excess of R3 000, you must be able to afford it.

Self-insurance: You do not have to insure everything you own. There are things you can replace cheaply, or you can build up a special savings account to insure yourself. Increasing your excess on a claim is a form of self-insurance.

Improve your security: The more you do to reduce the possibility of an insurance claim, such as not having your car parked on the street at night, the more your insurance company will like you and the more likely it will be to reduce your premiums.

No-claim bonuses: The less you claim, the less you will pay for short-term insurance. This particularly applies to motor vehicles. Always ask about no-claim bonuses.

Shop around: Different companies have different rates. There are special companies that will do the comparisons for you. However, you must check under what conditions a company will pay up. Most short-term policies have what are called exclusion clauses. Some of the exclusion clauses are there for good reason, for example letting someone without a driver's licence drive your car, or driving on smooth tyres. Others, however, can be ridiculous, such as not servicing your car precisely at every 10 000 kilometres. (I'm joking, but there are absurd exclusions. You must check your policy very carefully.)

CLAIMING ON SHORT-TERM INSURANCE

It is important that you report your loss to the insurance company as soon as possible. If you have been the victim of a theft or have been involved in a motor vehicle accident, you must also report the incident to the police. Your insurance company will want the police case or docket number. If there were witnesses to the loss or accident, take down their names and addresses, for the police as well as for the insurance company.

If you have been involved in an accident, write down the details and draw a picture illustrating the event as soon as you can, so that there is an accurate record of what happened. This is particularly the case when you are in the right and want to claim against someone else.

SOME WARNINGS

Never admit guilt: If you are in a motor vehicle accident, never admit that you are in the wrong. In some cases, if you admit guilt, the insurance company will not pay up. Although you may feel that you are in the wrong, you may not be. The other driver may have been drunk, driving a stolen car with smooth tyres without a driver's licence, and you may have thought you were in the wrong because you slammed on brakes for a tortoise crossing the road and the other driver hit you from behind.

Insure for the proper value: If you try to reduce your premiums by declaring the value of the items you want to insure as less than they actually are, you can get yourself into trouble. The insurance company, at worst, will refuse to pay your claim, because you lied about the value of your goods. At best, the insurance company will reduce the payout on your claim. For example, say you said that all your furniture and household effects were worth R40 000, but they were actually worth R60 000. This means that you are underinsured by R20 000, or 33 percent. If your television set was stolen and you claimed the full value of R3 000, an assessor (someone who checks on insurance claims) will make an assessment of your claim, which includes checking if you were underinsured. On finding that you are underinsured, your claim payout would be reduced by 33 percent. So, instead of getting R3 000, you would only be paid out R2 000.

LONG-TERM ASSURANCE (LIFE ASSURANCE)

The first thing to understand about life assurance is that it breaks into two parts, namely risk assurance against dying or being disabled; and investment. The investment side of life assurance is dealt with in Chapter Four.

Long-term risk assurance is also known as life and disability assurance. This means that for a monthly premium (payment) you can take a bet against a life assurance company about when you will die, or become disabled and unable to work. It's a bet that you don't really want to win. You only really need life assurance when you have people who depend on you to survive, for example when you are married and have children, or you have parents to support; or when you have high debt, such as a mortgage bond.

Disability assurance is something you need from the day you have to make your own living. The reason for this is that if you become disabled and are unable to work, you will still need money to live. There is often a snag with disability assurance, in that you will find it difficult to get disability assurance without it being linked to life assurance. When considering life and disability assurance, you must look at medical assurance (or medical aid).

HOW MUCH LIFE AND DISABILITY ASSURANCE DO YOU NEED?

Your need for life and disability assurance will vary at different times of your life. For example, when you have your own children and they still have to be educated, fed and clothed, you would increase the amount of life and disability assurance you have. The best type of life assurance is called term assurance. You can get term assurance for any period. At the end of the period the policy falls away. If you have not claimed, the life assurance company has won the bet and keeps your money. If you, or the people who depend on you, have claimed, you, unfortunately, have won the bet. However, do not see money you have spent on assurance as money lost. Think of the consequences if your parents had died in a car crash when you were 10 years old and had left no money for you.

The reasons why you need life and disability cover include:

- Being able to support yourself and any dependants if you are disabled and unable to work.
- Being able to support dependants if you die. Dependants may include elderly parents, a life partner and/or children. The dependency may also occur at a future date, for example with elderly parents.
- Ensuring that a business venture can continue. For example, if you own your own business or are in partnership with someone else, what would happen to the business if you died? Would there be sufficient money to keep the business viable?
- Covering estate duty and capital gains tax if you died.

There are ways of working out how much life and disability assurance you need by doing what is called a fact find or a financial needs analysis. Most insurance salespeople will have computer programs that will work out how much assurance you need. You can also access these programs yourself on the Internet. Computer programs can be manipulated. Be very careful about the information that is fed in. The most important figure is on inflation. Unscrupulous advisers will put very high inflation figures into the calculation to scare you out of your wits and bluff you into getting more life assurance than you need.

If you are already working and belong to a retirement scheme, you will usually also receive what are called group life and disability benefits. In effect, through your retirement scheme you are assured that if you die or become disabled, you or your dependants will be paid out. The amount by which you are covered (the amount that will be paid out) normally depends on how much you are earning and on the rules of the scheme. You need to find out what cover you have and take this into account when calculating any additional assurance needs you may have.

SHOP AROUND FOR LIFE AND DISABILITY ASSURANCE

Life and disability assurance premiums (what you pay) can and do differ from company to company. Before you take out life assurance, compare costs. For example, if you want life and disability assurance for R1 million, then find out how much each company will charge in monthly premiums and whether the premiums are guaranteed.

The premiums will depend on a number of factors that affect you. These include:

- **Your age:** The younger you are the cheaper your assurance will be, because you are not expected to die young and you may be paying for a longer time.
- **Your state of health:** If you are sickly you could well die earlier.
- **Your personal habits:** If you smoke and drink heavily your health will be undermined.
- **Your job and hobbies:** If you are employed as an undersea diver during the week and parachute jump at weekends, you can expect to pay more because of the dangers to your life.
- **Your lifestyle:** If you are in what is called a high-risk category (this means there is a high risk of you dying), you are likely to pay more. An example is someone who is a drug addict. Not only is there a risk of your taking an overdose, but drug addicts also fall into the high-risk area of contracting AIDS.

SOME WARNINGS

Tell the truth: Never, ever lie or keep quiet about facts that could affect the level of the premium you pay. If you give false or incorrect information knowingly and the life assurance company finds out, it will repudiate your claim. In other words, you will not be paid out. Rather pay a higher premium and know that there will be no trouble when you or your dependants claim. For example, if you suffer from severe asthma, you must declare this. Your premium may be a bit higher, but this is better than your dependants receiving nothing when you die.

Avoid the unnecessary: You will often see advertised what appears to be very cheap assurance for losing an eye/your big toe/an arm or being killed in an accident. You don't need it. The probability of ever making a claim on this type of insurance is negligible – and the people selling this type of assurance know it. Buy assurance that is based on your properly defined needs and those of any dependants you may have.

Avoid mixing risk and investment: Preferably avoid buying what is called a universal policy. This type of life assurance policy combines assurance investment with risk assurance. Risk assurance is another term to describe life and disability assurance, because there is a risk of you dying or becoming disabled. Life assurance products often come with the two combined. Life assurance salespeople will attempt to sell you the two combined, because they will often get a bigger commission. As a general rule you should not involve yourself in an investment scheme that ties you up for longer than 10 years.

The main reason why you should not link the two is that you never know what the future holds. You may lose your job and no longer be able to afford the combined premiums for the savings contract and the life assurance. You cannot easily separate the part of your premiums going towards investment and the part going towards risk assurance. The result is that if you stop paying premiums, you could lose your life assurance cover.

CREDIT LIFE ASSURANCE

Whenever you buy something big on credit (you borrow money), such as a car, you may be asked to take out life assurance to cover the amount of your debt. The purpose is to ensure that if you die your debt will be paid off. This is called credit life assurance. It is important that you take out this assurance if there will not be sufficient money to cover the debt when you die. This becomes particularly important if you have dependants who will face losing the asset or having to pay off the debt.

Often you will find that an unscrupulous salesperson will try to make the term (the number of years that the life assurance will be in force) longer than the period within which you must repay the debt. They may also attempt to add on investments. This is also nonsense and more in the interest of the salesperson, who will be earning a bigger commission, than in your interest.

Shop around. More often than not, credit life assurance offered to you directly by the person arranging your loan is more expensive than what you can get elsewhere. It is against the law to force you to buy credit life assurance from a particular company.

ESTATE PLANNING

Estate planning means having a plan for when the unexpected happens, such as being hit by a bus. Inextricably tied to life assurance, it is planning for what happens when the unexpected happens. Unfortunately it is not only the elderly who die. You need to have a plan for what happens when you die. Once you have assets and/or dependants, you must draw up a will to take care of your dependants and/or to distribute your assets to people (your heirs) who you want to have inherit from your estate (what you own).

Don't die without a will. Dying without a will is called dying intestate. If you die without a will, your estate (that is everything you own) is divided according to a formula that could see a cousin you loathe getting a slice of the pie. Dying intestate could also result in people who you would favour receiving less.

Although you can draw up a simple will stating, 'I leave all my earthly possessions to the Home for Stray Dogs,' life is normally a lot more complicated, and you should get advice and assistance in drawing up a will to avoid later problems. Lawyers and banks will draw up wills. In most cases you will not pay a fee, because the lawyer or executor will collect a fee of 3.5 percent of your assets when you die for ensuring that the terms of the will are met.

It is important that your will spells out how, when and under what conditions your assets should be divided after your death. Your estate can be divided in a number of ways. This includes creating an income stream from your capital for an heir, to merely leaving everything as a lump sum to an heir or beneficiary to your will.

MEDICAL ASSURANCE

Medical assurance is just as important as life assurance. Medical costs can be enormous, and could put you very badly into debt. If you have a job, most employers provide you with medical assurance, usually through what is called a medical aid scheme.

There are two main types of medical aid schemes, namely restricted schemes and open schemes. Most restricted schemes are either sponsored by an employer or by groups, such as unions or employers' bodies involved in a particular industry, e.g. bankers.

Employers often make it compulsory to be a member of a medical scheme – either a restricted scheme or an open scheme recognised by the company. In such cases the company normally pays a subsidy in the form of part of the contribution.

If you are self-employed, you can also join an 'open' medical aid scheme.

No two schemes are the same. Open and closed schemes have different contribution and benefit levels. Obviously, if you have to be a member of a restricted scheme your choices are likely to be limited.

All medical schemes are subject to the Medical Schemes Act. In terms of the Act you cannot be refused membership of an open medical scheme. However, if you do not work for an employer you can be refused membership of a closed scheme.

You cannot be kicked off your medical aid scheme willy-nilly. If you are a member of a medical scheme of any type you cannot be dumped if you become ill or old. If you are married, your spouse and dependants can continue membership after your death. Once you have joined a fund, the benefits carry on until death if you continue to pay your contributions. Other important legal issues include:

- **Waiting periods:** Waiting periods can be applied, at the discretion of the scheme, when you join a scheme, particularly for pre-existing conditions. These periods are:
    - A general maximum waiting period of three months, during which time you will not be able to make any claims;
    - Nine months for pregnancy. In other words, you cannot be pregnant when you are accepted for membership; and
    - Up to 12 months for any specific existing illness or medical condition.
- **Late joiner penalties:** If you have not been a member of a scheme before the age of 35, penalty fees can be applied. The penalties are back-dated to the age of 30. The longer you wait before joining a scheme, the higher the penalties will be. If you were previously a member of another scheme, any years of membership will be subtracted from your current age, and the resulting age band and penalty rate will be determined on that basis. In other words, age at application minus years of creditable coverage.

    You have to provide proof of previous membership. The proof can be provided at any stage, and when provided the new scheme must recalculate the penalty.

- **Community rating:** This means that all members must be charged the same. The only factors that can alter how much you pay is your level of income and the number of dependants you have.
- **Contributions/benefits:** The contribution (what you pay for membership) and benefit (what is paid out to you) levels of schemes can be altered. There is no law or regulation that prescribes maximum contributions, but there are regulations that stipulate minimum benefits. These benefits include treatment for AIDS at a public hospital.

    You also need to be aware that with an employer-sponsored closed scheme your employer can alter their contributions, depending on the rules of the scheme and employment contracts with employees.

CHOICES

There is an increasing variety of choices that are being made available in medical schemes. The choices break down into three main areas: traditional schemes, managed schemes and new generation schemes. There are fundamental differences between the three choices.

1. TRADITIONAL MEDICAL SCHEMES

Until recently all medical aids worked in much the same way. The basics are:

- Contributions: If it is an employer scheme, both you and your employer contribute; or if you are self-employed, you alone contribute. The amount you pay each month is based on your level of pay and the number of dependants you have. (The number of claims you have or your state of health is not taken into consideration for contribution purposes.)
- Claims: Claims procedures are complex and vary from scheme to scheme. They include:
  - RAMS: Most schemes pay between 80 and 100 percent of what is called the Rates of Medical Societies (RAMS). These are rates set down by the Association of Medical Aids. However, not many doctors stick to these rates (and they are not obliged to). If your doctor is not a member of RAMS, then you have to pay the difference between what you would have paid under a normal RAMS rate and the rate charged by your doctor. Example: Say you consulted your doctor and you were charged R200. The RAMS rate is R140. You can claim 80 percent of your doctor's bill on the RAMS rate. So you would pay the R60 difference

between the two rates plus the 20 percent of R140 (R28). Your share would be R88. Your medical aid would pay R112.
- Caps: Every year you are given limits on how much you may claim. Say you are allowed to claim R15 000 a year: once you have passed that point you would have to pay everything. With most schemes there are limits on dentist's bills, glasses, ordinary doctors, hospital bills, etc.
- Exclusions: Many schemes will not pay out for certain medical bills. For example, if you want plastic surgery to alter the size or shape of your nose, it is highly unlikely a medical scheme will pay up. Many schemes also refuse to pay for some things you would expect them to pay for, such as birth control pills. The same scheme will, however, be prepared to pay out thousands of rands for the birth of a child!

Always check all the conditions – particularly what you may or may not claim for – of any medical scheme. You may find that you will need to buy additional medical assurance.

2. MANAGED HEALTHCARE

Managed healthcare comes in many different shapes and forms. Agreements are reached with healthcare providers, such as doctors and hospitals. The agreements include costs and level of health service provided. The care providers range from doctors, to pharmacies, to hospitals. In the past, a major criticism of managed care schemes by members was that they were given little freedom of choice of healthcare service provider, and as a result could receive substandard care. Although there is now greater freedom of choice and patient control, you are, however, in most cases still restricted to choosing from the panels provided by the managed care system. The upside is cost containment.

Managed schemes are often attached to other new generation funding vehicles, so you should compare schemes. The issues you should compare in managed healthcare include:

- Contribution levels;
- Benefits. These are not only limited to the amounts paid out, but also include various quirks such as, if you are hospitalised, whether the scheme pays out for each day in hospital, or whether you have to be admitted for, say, three days before you can claim;
- The network structure. For example, how many hospitals are included from which you can choose, and where are they? If you are ill you do not

want to be admitted to a hospital many kilometres away; and
- Choice of healthcare service providers, such as doctors and dentists.

3. NEW GENERATION SCHEMES

1. TRADITIONAL MEDICAL SCHEMES

2. MANAGED HEALTHCARE

3. NEW GENERATION SCHEMES

Most of the new generation medical schemes are based on the principle of reducing cross-subsidisation and getting you to save now for the likelihood of poor health when you are older. The structures are being changed in order to get rid of many of the problems of traditional schemes, such as over-claiming.

The new generation schemes are designed to be tax efficient, put the onus on you to control your own medical costs and give you rewards for keeping down claims and costs.

The fundamentals of new generation schemes

There are three legs to the new generation schemes which, among other things, dramatically reduce cross-subsidies between the young and healthy and the old and unhealthy, and which will hopefully keep costs down. These are:

- Savings schemes: You put a certain amount aside every month in what is effectively an interest-earning savings account, on which you draw to pay for day-to-day medical needs, such as influenza injections. If you do not use all the money in one year, your contributions are reduced for the next year;
- High-cost cover: You virtually buy assurance for high-cost critical medical needs and major calamities, such as hospitalisation;
- Investing for the future: Funds similar to retirement provident funds are established so that you can save for higher medical costs, which you will more than likely face when you retire;
- Options: Most new generation schemes offer various options, from very simple schemes with comparatively lower contributions, which cover you for high-cost health events; through to comprehensive options with high levels of contributions, which provide cover for everything from chronic medicines through to hospitalisation. You need to be careful that when you join a low-cost option, it will not be exorbitantly expensive when you need a higher level of cover.

You need to compare the schemes that you are offered. For example, you must know what is covered by your savings account for day-to-day expenses, and what is considered to be a major cost. For example, some schemes will pay for your hospitalisation after a motor vehicle accident, but expect you to pay for physiotherapy while you are recovering.

Health assurance is very complex and is changing all the time. You should take your time in reaching a decision about what scheme suits you best, but remember that it is not a choice of whether you should or should not have medical assurance: it is a matter of getting the most affordable scheme to meet your needs.

GETTING ADVICE ON INSURANCE

Advice on insurance is important, but you must be sure that you are getting the right advice from properly trained people who are acting in your best interests.

DO YOU NEED ADVICE?

Often you do not need much advice. For example, on short-term insurance, if you know how it works, you read books such as this one and your family and friends discuss the issues, you can probably do without advice.

If you go without advice, you must do your homework very carefully. You will need to check with the various insurance companies on their charges (premiums) and conditions. Some insurance as well as life assurance companies, which try to protect their sales force, do not like you doing business directly and will try to put you off.

However, there are an increasing number of companies, particularly in short-term insurance, that do business directly, mainly over the telephone.

The same applies to life assurance and even investments. If your needs are simple – for example, buying credit life assurance – then try to deal direct.

And again, the same applies to investment. If you are investing a comparatively small amount of money every month, decide on one or two unit trusts and contact the unit trust company directly. When you invest directly, you should enquire about discounts for not working through a broker.

However, if you are unsure of yourself or have complicated affairs, such as having dependants for whom you must provide, then you should consult a financial adviser.

A FEW GUIDELINES

When you feel you need guidance on insurance and investment, choose the person who represents you very carefully. Financial advisers go by many different names, including intermediaries, financial planners, brokers and agents. You need to take the following issues into account when choosing a financial adviser:

- **Long-term relationship:** A financial adviser is involved in an important aspect of your life, much like a doctor or a dentist. They get to know things about you that you may not discuss with your closest friends. So you need a trusting, long-term relationship.
- **What type:** You can choose between someone who is an independent financial adviser, who sells the products of a large number of companies; an agent who only sells the products of one company; or a general agent who is employed by a specific company, but can sell the products of other companies that have been approved by his company. Independent financial advisers have the advantage of being able to give you more choice, while agents have the backing of their companies in giving you advice, and if something goes wrong with the advice you can take it up with the employing company.
- **Not a one-person show:** Select a financial advice company that has a number of people working for it. Financial services are becoming so complex, the more brains you have working for you the better.
- **Speak to more than one person:** Find out the names of financial advisers from friends and relatives. Draw up a shortlist and meet them. Find out from them what they can offer you. Do not be put off by the fact that you are young and may not have much money. A good adviser will be looking at a relationship in the years ahead when you could be very wealthy (hopefully on the basis of good advice from him or her).
- **Qualifications and experience:** Anyone can become a financial adviser without any qualifications or knowledge. Find out details about qualifications and experience. If you can find someone who is, for example, a Certified Financial Planner (CFP) accredited to the Financial Planning Institute of South Africa, then at least you know you have someone who is highly qualified.
- **Neighbourhood:** If the person lives and has been living in your neighbourhood for a while then it is a good sign, as the person is quite happy to associate with people with whom he has done good, and not bad business.

- **Payment:** Establish how the adviser is paid. If you can find someone that you pay only by fees, that is the best way to go. Upfront commission payments are the most dangerous, as once the adviser has sold you the product you may never hear from them again.
- **Ask questions:** It is your money. Don't be shy about asking questions – you are putting your hard-won savings on the table. Protect them.

GETTING FAIR TREATMENT

Some insurance companies will do everything they can not to pay claims. If you feel you are not being justly treated you can contact an ombudsman. An ombudsman is appointed to resolve disputes quickly and cheaply. There is no cost to you for taking a complaint to the ombudsman.

The Ombudsman for Long-Term Assurance: PO Box 4967, Cape Town 8000

The Ombudsman for Short-Term Insurance: PO Box 30619, Johannesburg 1000

12

Paying Tax

Unfortunately, taxation is going to play a major part in your life. If you are already working, either full time or part time, you are probably already seeing the effects of taxation on your income. You are never too young to pay tax. You became a taxpayer on the first day that you spent money, because nearly every time you buy something you pay tax.

Taxes are used to pay for many things. The money pays for schools, libraries, hospitals, roads, dams, the police force, the army and national parks and forests. Taxes are used to pay the salaries of all the people who work for the government and to help the very poor. If you have very many poor people in society, who see no chance of improving their position, crime is likely to be high. So, although it may hurt to pay your taxes, think of all the good that can be done with your money and the services you use every day, such as roads.

Unfortunately South Africa has what is called a low tax base. This means that only a small proportion of people are paying tax, because so many people are without jobs or earn low incomes. The result is that a limited number of taxpayers have to pay quite a lot of what they earn in taxes. It also means the government cannot do all the things it would like to do to improve the living conditions of all South Africans.

The problem of a low tax base in South Africa has been made worse by the fact that there is a low tax morality as well. That is, many people do everything they can to avoid paying taxes. However, the South African Revenue Service (SARS) has in recent years become a lot more efficient, and is now starting to track down tax cheats. If you deliberately avoid paying taxes, you can face very heavy fines and even go to jail.

Taxes are collected in many different ways and at different levels of government.

LOCAL GOVERNMENT TAXES

At the lowest level, people who own property must pay taxes to their local authority. These are called rates. Property rates are set on the value of the property and the value of the buildings on the property.

CENTRAL GOVERNMENT TAXES

Most taxes are collected for the central government by the South African Revenue Service (SARS). Most taxes are decided on each year when the Minister of Finance presents Parliament with the budget in a special speech, called the Budget Speech.

The Minister tells Parliament how much money will be required to run all the services for the forthcoming year and how he will get the money to pay the bills. It is much like your budget – there are just many more entries and a lot more money is involved. Most of the money to pay the bills will come from taxes. Members of parliament will spend many weeks discussing the budget of the government and many changes will be suggested, some of which will be accepted and others rejected. In the end, all members of parliament must vote to reject or accept the budget.

Democracy has its roots in taxation. The first parliaments were established because people, who were paying the taxes, demanded that they be given a say in the spending of their taxes. Not everyone could attend a meeting to make the decisions on how to spend taxes, so it was decided that large groups should elect representatives (now known as members of parliament). In the early days of democracy, only people who paid taxes were allowed to vote. Nowadays, nearly everyone above the age of 18 is allowed to vote. The reason for this is that if people who did not pay taxes could not vote, the elected representatives of the people would not worry about them. No tax money would be spent on non-taxpayers, and the position of non-voting, non-taxpayers would become worse and worse.

Deciding on the budget is the most important thing that members of parliament do. This is also why it is important that when you vote in elections for a government, you understand the economic policies of the various political parties. A political party's economic policy, in simple terms, means the way the party wants to collect taxes and spend the money.

Two Main Ways To Collect Tax

There are two main ways that you will pay tax. One way is called direct taxation. This is tax that you normally have to pay directly to the taxman and is based on money you receive. The other is called indirect taxation, which is normally collected by someone else and is based on money you spend.

DIRECT TAXATION

There are eight facts you need to take into account with direct taxation:

1. REGISTERING AS A TAXPAYER

The responsibility to register as a taxpayer is on you. Most employers will normally help you register if you are working for the first time. If not, look up the address of your local office of the SARS, and send the taxman a letter asking them to register you as a taxpayer. When you are registered you will be given a tax number, which will stick with you for the rest of your life. You can be prosecuted for not registering as a taxpayer.

Every year you will be sent what is called a tax return to fill in. If you earn more than a minimum amount (the amount changes every year) and/or you have any income that comes from any other source apart from wages or salaries, such as returns from an investment, you will have to complete a tax return.

2. INCOME TAX

Income tax is based on how much you earn (income), hence the name income tax. If you are employed and are paid a salary every month, you will find one, if not two, types of tax deducted from your pay. It does not matter how old you are – if you earn income from any source, you are liable to pay income tax. Whether you are working over the school holidays, or you are an orphan who has income from money left to you by your parents, you are liable for income tax.

Many employers do not bother to deduct income tax from people they employ casually, particularly during vacations. However, this will differ from employer to employer.

Income tax is divided into two parts if you are employed, namely Standard Income Tax on Employees, or SITE; and Pay As You Earn, or PAYE.

SITE: If you earn below a certain level, you will only pay SITE. In the 2002 tax year, if you earned less than R60 000, you only paid SITE. The tax is automatically deducted from what you are paid by your employer. Generally you cannot get a refund for SITE, unless your employer has not taken account of any contributions you may have made to a retirement fund or medical aid plan.

The big advantage of being a SITE-only taxpayer is that you do not have to fill in tax forms every year, unless you earn money from another source, such as from investments.

PAYE: Over the cut-off level for SITE you will also pay PAYE. The big difference between SITE and PAYE is that at the end of February and before the end of May, every year, you have to fill in a tax form telling the taxman how much you have earned and how much tax you have paid. The taxman then decides if you have paid too much or too little. If you have paid too much you get some money back, and sadly you have to pay money in if you did not pay enough tax.

Provisional Income Tax: If you are self-employed or earn more than R10 000 a year from sources apart from an employer, such as interest on investments, you may have to register with SARS as a provisional taxpayer. If you are a provisional taxpayer you have to pay in tax a few times a year. The reason for this is that there is no automatic system such as PAYE to deduct income tax from what you earn.

With provisional tax you must make three payments. These payments are:

- A first payment that is due within the first six months of the tax year, and which must be equal to one-half of your estimated income tax for the year. The amount may not be lower than the previous year without the permission of SARS.

- A second payment that is due on or before the last day of the tax year (February 28). The amount must be equal to the estimated tax due for the year, less what you have already paid. If you are more than 10 percent out in your estimation, you will pay a penalty of 20 percent on any underpaid amount, plus interest.
- A third voluntary payment, payable within seven months of the end of the tax year, allows you to make good any incorrect estimation.

3. NOT EVERYONE MUST PAY TAX

If you earn less than R27 000 a year (the 2002 amount) you do not have to pay income tax. If you are working part time and your employer is deducting SITE, but you are earning less than R27 000 a year, you must ask your employer to get a tax directive from the local tax office stating that tax will not be deducted from your earnings. You must check the new threshold every year.

4. DEDUCTIONS

There are a number of deductions that you can make from your taxable income. These include:

- Most expenses involved in generating the income;
- Contributions to retirement funds, within defined limits; and
- Medical expenses, within limits.

You deduct these amounts before you calculate how much tax you must pay.

5. INCOME TAX RATES

South Africa, in common with most countries, has what is called a progressive personal income tax system. To give you a very simple example of what this means: Say you earned R1 000 for the year, and the tax rate on R1 000 was 10 percent. You would then pay R10.00 in tax.

Now here comes the progressive step. Say you earned R2 000. The second step (or marginal rate) may be 15 percent. However, you still only pay 10 percent on the first R1 000 you earned in the year. The 15 percent applies only to the second R1 000 you earn. You can never pay a higher rate on that first R1 000. Here is how you would do the calculation on this simplified example:

INCOME	MARGINAL TAX RATE	TAX PAYABLE
First R1 000	10%	R100
Second R1 000	15%	R150
Total Tax Paid:		**R250**

A Fallacy

You will often hear people claiming that they receive less income (pay) in total when they receive a salary increase, because they went into a higher tax bracket. This is not possible, because you always pay the same amount on the previous rand. It is the additional rands that you earn in a particular bracket on which you pay more.

Marginal rate of taxation

There are six marginal tax brackets, which were structured for the 2002/3 tax year, like this:

TAXABLE INCOME		RATES OF TAX
Exceeds	**But does not exceed**	
(Rand)	**(Rand)**	
zero	40 000	18% of each rand
40 001	80 000	7 200 + 25% on any rand in excess of R 40 000
80 001	110 000	17 200 + 30% on any rand in excess of R 80 000
110 001	170 000	26 200 + 35% on any rand in excess of R110 000
170 001	240 000	47 200 + 38% on any rand in excess of R170 000
240 001	–	73 800 + 40% on any rand in excess of R240 000

Simple example of a tax calculation

Someone earning R88 000 a year would pay:

Tax on R80 001:	R17 200
Plus 30% of R7 999:	R 2 399
Total Tax Due:	**R19 599**

6. AVERAGE RATE OF TAXATION

The average rate of taxation is the average amount of tax you pay on your income. For example, with an income of R240 001 you would be in the top marginal rate of 40 percent, but your average rate of taxation would be 30.74 percent. In other words, after averaging out all the different amounts you pay in the various marginal rate tax brackets, you would pay R73 800 in tax (before rebates).

You can calculate your average rate by using the following equation:

$$\frac{\text{Total tax paid} \times 100}{\text{Taxable Income}} = XX\%$$

Here are a few examples of average tax for a person under 65 (the primary rebate is excluded in the calculations, which are based on the 2002/3 tax tables).

TAXABLE INCOME Rand	TAX PAYABLE Rand	MARGINAL Rate %	AVERAGE Rate %
R 27 000	R 4 860	18	18
R 40 000	R 7 200	18	18
R 45 000	R 8 449	25	18.77
R 50 000	R 9 700	25	19.4
R 60 000	R12 200	25	20.33
R 70 000	R14 700	25	21
R 80 000	R17 200	25	21.5
R 90 000	R20 200	30	22.44
R100 000	R23 200	30	23.2
R120 000	R29 700	35	24.75
R160 000	R43 700	35	27.31
R200 000	R58 600	38	29.3
R250 000	R77 800	40	31.12

7. REBATES

There are rebates that are given against the tax that you must pay each year. There is a primary rebate for every taxpayer, and a secondary rebate (additional to the primary rebate) for people over the age of 65. For 2002/3 the tax rebates were R4 860 for the primary rebate, and R3 000 for the secondary rebate.

Once you have calculated how much tax you must pay, you then subtract the rebates to establish how much tax you will actually pay.

An example: Someone who is younger than 65, earning R88 000 a year:

Tax:	R19 599
Less Primary Rebate	R 4 860
Total Tax Due:	**R14 739**

8. CAPITAL GAINS TAX

Capital gains tax (CGT) was introduced in South Africa on 1 October 2001. No capital gain made before that date is subject to the new tax. In reality, capital gains tax is part of income tax. What happens is that 25 percent of any capital gain you make, with a few exceptions and an annual exemption on the first R10 000 capital gain, is subject to income tax.

Example:

Cost of asset:	R200 000
Sale of asset:	R300 000
Capital gain:	R100 000
25% of gain subject to CGT:	R 25 000
Less exemption:	R 10 000
Subject to CGT:	R 15 000

So, R15 000 will be added to your income for the year, and the amount will be taxed at your marginal rate.

You do not pay capital gains tax merely because an asset has increased in value. You need to have disposed of the asset.

There are a number of issues to take into account with capital gains tax.

1. Keep good records

You must keep good records on any asset you acquire, whether you believe it is subject to CGT or not. For example, although the first R1 million capital gain upon the disposal of your primary residence may be exempt from CGT while you live in it and use it exclusively for domestic purposes, this may not always be the case. In the future you may move out and let it, or you may use part of it for business purposes. This would result in part of the gain, on disposal of the property, becoming taxable. You need to keep proper records of:

- The cost or value at acquisition of all assets (keep all receipts and invoices).
- The date of acquisition of the assets.
- The cost or value of any additions to the assets.
- The date of any additions to the assets, e.g. improvements to your home or the purchase of additional unit trusts.
- The cost or value at disposal of the assets.
- The date of disposal of the assets.
- Portions of an asset used for business and private purposes.
- Periods of absence from a primary residence exceeding six months.

2. Did a CGT event occur during the tax year?

You need not have bought or sold an asset to be liable for CGT. A CGT event occurs when what is called a disposal (not necessarily a sale) of an asset that you have acquired (not necessarily bought) takes place. Events that are regarded as acquisitions of assets include:

- Purchase of an asset.
- Receiving an asset as a gift or donation.
- Inheriting an asset.

Events regarded as disposals of assets that may be subject to CGT include:

- A donation (except to public benefit organisations); expropriation (unless the proceeds are used to replace the assets within three years); conversion; cession (except where the asset has been ceded to a bank as security or as part of a divorce settlement); or transfer of ownership (except from one spouse to another). A portion of donations tax that you pay is deductible from the capital gain.
- The change of ownership on emigration, whether the asset is sold or not, except immovable property, which is taxed when sold.
- The asset's forfeiture, termination, redemption, cancellation, surrender, scrapping, loss or destruction.
- The transfer of an asset to a trust, or the vesting of an asset in a beneficiary of a trust (that is, the disposal of the asset to a beneficiary).

3. Is the asset exempt?

There are a number of assets that are excluded from CGT. These include:

- The first R1 million of gain or loss on the disposal of your primary residence.
- Personal-use assets, such as personal effects, jewellery, artworks, furniture and vehicles not used for trade purposes. Items such as gold coins and boats exceeding 10 metres in length are not considered personal effects.
- Any retirement savings investments, both pre- and post-retirement. There is a moratorium on retirement assets for three years.
- Profits made on life assurance policies (the CGT will have been paid on your behalf by the life assurance company), with the exception of second-hand policies, on which any gain or loss in your hands will be liable for CGT.
- Any gains as a result of compensation for personal injury, illness or defamation.
- Gains or losses made from any foreign currency left over from your travel allowance.
- Gains or losses made from any legal South African gambling, including the Lotto.
- Donations to public benefit organisations, such as charities and educational institutions.
- A transfer of assets between spouses or partners.

4. Consolidation of gains and losses

The total of your capital losses in any one tax year must be subtracted from the total of your capital gains. You cannot transfer capital losses between companies or trusts to reduce a gain made in a company or in your personal capacity. If you have made an overall loss, you may not deduct that loss from your taxable income for the year. The loss must be carried forward to a year when you make a capital gain. The loss can only be deducted against a future gain.

5. The exemption

Every year you are given a R10 000 exemption. The reason for this exemption is so that the taxman can avoid unnecessary work, especially in dealing with people below the income tax threshold who do not have to complete tax returns.

If you have a net capital loss, you cannot add the R10 000 exemption to the amount to make a greater loss, nor can you create a loss by deducting the R10 000 from a gain below R10 000. For example, if you have a net gain of R8 000 before the deduction of the R10 000 exemption, your gain will be reduced to zero, not to a loss of R2 000.

It is important to note that the annual exemption of R10 000 reduces both gains and losses. If the sum of your gains and losses for the year is a loss of R12 000, this will be reduced by R10 000, leaving a R2 000 loss to be carried forward to future tax years. If the net loss was R8 000, this would be reduced to zero.

If you know you are going to make a loss on the disposal of an asset, you should sell it either in the same year or in the year before you dispose of an asset on which there will be a capital gain. That way you will not see your assessed capital loss being eaten away by inflation. The exemption is increased to R50 000 in the year of assessment in which you die.

TRANSFER TAXES

Transfer taxes are direct taxes levied on assets that are transferred from one person to another. The main transfer taxes are: .

Estate duty: This is a tax that is paid on all your assets when you die. It is only payable if your assets are worth more than R1.5 million. The only time this tax is not paid is when married people leave their assets to the surviving partner. So, if your Dad died and left everything to your mother, no estate duty would be paid. But when they both die and leave their assets to you, then estate duty would have to be paid. The rate of taxation is 20 percent of every rand in excess of R1.5 million.

Property transfer taxes: Every time a property or home is sold, a tax is placed on the sale price of the property. In some ways this is also an indirect tax.

Donations tax: Any donation over R30 000 a year is taxed at 20 percent a year. So, if you are given R40 000 by your parents, they (not you) will have to pay donations tax of R2 000 on R10 000 of the amount. The only exception is to registered charities and educational institutions.

INDIRECT TAXES

As with direct taxes, indirect taxes also come in different forms. Indirect tax is a tax that you do not pay directly from your income. Normally an indirect tax is based on what you spend, and you are not responsible for seeing that it is given to the taxman. Indirect taxes include:

VALUE ADDED TAX (VAT)

VAT is the most common form of indirect tax. VAT is added to almost everything on which you spend money, whether they are goods or a service. The VAT rate is 14 percent. There are a few exceptions, including some basic foods, mainly to help the very poor. VAT is normally paid over to the taxman by the seller of the goods or the service provider. You do not have to worry about its collection or fill in any forms.

FUEL LEVY

For every litre of petrol you buy, you are paying a levy to the government. Originally this levy was intended to pay for better roads, but now it goes into the general government pot. You also pay VAT on this tax.

IMPORT TAXES

These taxes are paid on a wide range of goods that are imported from other countries. Often these taxes are used to protect South African industries so that something bought cheaply overseas cannot be sold in South Africa for less than it costs to make the same article here. The tax is also placed on luxury goods to make them even more expensive, so that they do not find many buyers in South Africa. We have to send money overseas for all the imported goods we buy. This weakens our economy.

LUXURY OR AD VALOREM TAXES

These taxes are added to a wide variety of goods. Two of the most notorious are the taxes on booze and smoking, also called sin taxes.

If you have any problems or are not sure what to do, telephone or write to your local SARS office. The taxman is obliged to help you and give you the right information about what tax you must pay and what costs you can claim.

13

Working Abroad

Increasingly, South Africans, unable to find jobs locally and not having sufficient capital to start a business, are looking to foreign countries to build savings and/or get work experience. With the exchange rate strongly in favour of earning foreign currency, others are also taking a few years to build up savings to give them a quick start back in South Africa (e.g. enabling them to buy property).

A recent example I came across – let's call her Jan – moved to London after graduating. She saved £400 in her first month, which translates into more than R6 200 ... probably close to what she would have earned if she had been able to find a job in South Africa. Multiply that by 24 months, and she could return with as much as R150 000. There are not many young South Africans who could save that much as quickly at home.

Many South Africans abroad are saving even more than Jan – particularly those who are doing both day and evening jobs.

Another example: A portfolio manager, who works for a large South African financial services company, spent two years in Britain with his wife and, between them, accumulated about R1 million in two years.

At the same time, the experience acquired abroad is invaluable when it comes to finding a job back home.

Although it is tempting to see your foreign earnings translated into bags of rands, there is no longer any obligation to return the money to South Africa if you don't need it immediately. If you want to leave it behind, though, it would be wise to invest the money in an offshore investment offering, such as a unit trust fund (called a mutual fund in every other country in the world).

But be sure that you understand what is meant by offshore. There is a difference between a foreign and an offshore investment. An offshore investment is through a jurisdiction where there is no or low tax on investments. The best offshore centres to use are the Channel Islands, the Isle of Man and Dublin. If you can anticipate that you'll be doing this, you should take this route from the start, so that you do not have to cash an investment, say in London, to transfer it to an offshore centre when you leave.

With your investment offshore, you are liable for tax on any income generated by the investment in the UK while you are working there, and in South Africa when you return. But, if you leave the investment in London, you could be subject to tax both in South Africa and London upon your return.

When making the investment, you should also consider using a South African company. This makes administration easier in the long term, and most of South Africa's major financial institutions have offices and investment products in the main offshore centres.

TAX

If you are not resident in South Africa, you are not obliged to pay South African tax on the money you earn while you are resident in another country, as long as you are not in South Africa for more than 180 days of any tax year. If you are resident in South Africa for longer than that period, in most cases you will be able to deduct any tax you have paid overseas from any tax you owe in South Africa on your foreign earnings. When you return to South Africa, the capital amount of any money you bring in will not be subject to income or capital gains tax.

If you leave money overseas, you will have to declare this to the tax authorities, as well as any earnings or capital gains you make. But there are snags to working abroad. Admission to another country is not automatic, particularly if you do not have access to a foreign passport.

Britain and the United States are the favourite targets of people seeking jobs, because both countries have programmes that allow young people from other countries to take working holidays there – but if either country suspects for one moment that your intentions are something beyond a working holiday, you won't be allowed in.

If you have a foreign passport, particularly a European Union passport, it is virtually 'open sesame'. You can enter any European Union country with a passport belonging to a European Union country and stay as long as you like. Most European Union passports also make access to the United States easier.

If you don't have ancestral or citizen rights you have no automatic right to other visas. The issuing of visas is completely at the discretion of the host country. Even if you receive a visa, you can still be turned back when you enter the country of your destination if immigration officials believe that you may not stick to the conditions attached to your visa. It has become increasingly difficult for young males to obtain special visas, because it is suspected that they may overstay their welcome.

UNITED KINGDOM

Many parts of London, such as the Wimbledon–Southfields–Putney area, often seem more like a twelfth province of South Africa. Apart from the South African accents that predominate at the Underground stations and local pubs, you can buy Mrs Ball's chutney and peppermint crisps in many of the local supermarkets.

London has become the main destination for many of South Africa's educated jobless and adventure seekers. The reason is that it is one of the easiest countries for South Africans to get into since South Africa rejoined the Commonwealth, and also because many South Africans can claim ancestral citizenship rights.

There are a number of ways to get into the United Kingdom: with a European Union passport (no visa required); an ancestral visa; a working visa; or a working holiday visa.

WORKING HOLIDAY VISA

A working holiday visa is issued for a maximum of two years and can be withdrawn at any stage if you have not adhered to the conditions.

To qualify for a working holiday visa you must meet the following conditions:

- You must be a Commonwealth citizen (South Africa was readmitted to the Commonwealth in 1994).
- You must be aged between 17 and 27.
- You must have a return air ticket (but don't buy the ticket before you get the visa).
- You need to be able to prove that you will not become financially dependent on the British state. In most cases you are required to show that you have at least R25 000 in the bank in South Africa.
- You can be married or unmarried, but if married, both partners must meet the requirements for a working visa individually.
- You may have dependent children, but they must be under the age of five and must not reach the age of five while you are in the United Kingdom.
- You must state that you will only undertake jobs that are incidental to a working holiday, and that you will not be seeking to further your own career in your chosen profession. If you have qualified with a BComm, it will be suspicious if you start applying for a banking or accountancy job. A working holiday visa holder cannot take up managerial positions or act as a locum hospital doctor, general practitioner or lawyer, or be a professional sportsperson or entertainer. To quote from British High Commission documentation: 'Working holiday-makers can only do part-time casual work of less than 25 hours per week for the full duration of their stay in the United Kingdom or full-time work for half the duration.' Also, you may not have financial commitments in Britain, such as a mortgage bond on property, or a car or student loan, that will require you to earn a regular wage. All this does not mean that many South Africans on working visas do not do jobs in line with their qualifications. They do. The important thing is not to show that you are intending to do this. For example, you should not start applying for jobs in line with your qualifications while you are still in South Africa. If the immigration authorities at Heathrow Airport find any evidence in a quick search that you have or are intending to find a job to further your career, you will be on the first aircraft back to South Africa (without any refund on your ticket).
- You must be able to show that you intend to return to South Africa. This can include a commitment to further study or a letter from a potential employer that you will be offered a job on your return.
- You must have a passport that is valid for at least six months.

You may apply for a second two-year working visa at the expiry of your first working holiday visa, but will have to show that you have adhered to the conditions of the first visa.

You are permitted to study in the United Kingdom while you have a working holiday visa, but you will have to show that you will be able to pay the study fees.

How to apply

You need to apply to the consular section of the British High Commission in Pretoria. You can contact the High Commission in Pretoria at 012 483 1402, or visit the website, www.britain.org.za, where you can download visa application forms. The High Commission provides a full set of application forms and precise instructions about applying for the visa. The list of questions is extensive and is aimed mainly at establishing that you are going on a working holiday and will be returning to South Africa.

You may also be required to go to the High Commission in Pretoria for an interview if the consular section suspects that your application for a working visa may not be genuine.

A WORKING VISA

If you want to work in the United Kingdom in your chosen profession or as a professional sportsperson or entertainer, you and your prospective employer will have to apply for a work visa. This type of visa has its own conditions and limitations, which differ from applicant to applicant. You need to contact the British High Commission in Pretoria for details, or the London-based Immigration Advisory Service, which is a charitable body. The IAS can be contacted at ++44 20 7357 7511; or e-mail: advice@ias.org; or website: www.iasuk.org.

Generally an employer will have to show that they are unable to fill the position with a British or European Union citizen, and that you are the only person with the right skills and experience available to fill the vacancy.

To qualify you must have a degree (with work experience); or a relevant diploma (with no work experience); or a general diploma (with at least one year of work experience); or, if you have no tertiary qualifications, you must have three years' specialist work experience.

A work permit is valid for five years. After you have completed four years, you can apply for permanent residence. If you change jobs before the expiry of your permit or before you have permanent residence, your new employer will have to apply for a new work visa on your behalf.

AN ANCESTRY VISA

An ancestry visa gives you far more scope to live and work in the United Kingdom. To qualify:

- You must be at least 17 years old.
- You must be a citizen of a Commonwealth country.
- You must have a grandparent born in the United Kingdom. This includes the Channel Islands, the Isle of Man and a grandparent born in the Republic of Ireland before 31 March 1922.
- You must be able to work and will seek employment in the United Kingdom (i.e. you do not intend to live on the dole – the national welfare system).
- You must be able to meet the costs of your daily living.

The visas are for four years and are subject to you spending a minimum amount of time in Britain. After you have completed four years, you can apply for permanent residence. You are entitled to do any job you choose.

RIGHT OF ABODE

If you or one of your parents was born in the United Kingdom, you may apply for a Certificate of Entitlement to the Right of Abode. The Right of Abode is valid for the life of your passport and entitles you to live and do any job in the United Kingdom for as long as you like.

SOME USEFUL ADVICE

Britain is a hi-tech society, and almost everything you need to know from jobs to accommodation can be found on the Internet. There are plenty of sites aimed particularly at young South Africans, Aussies and Kiwis.

It is worth visiting these websites even before you leave South Africa. Some of the more useful sites are: www.chillitree.co.uk; www.thegumtree.com; www.1stcontact.co.uk; www:citylets.com. When in Britain, *TNT* magazine is a useful source of information.

UNITED STATES OF AMERICA

The United States provides various types of visas for work and cultural experience to young people. Since the 11 September attacks on the World Trade Center in New York, the US has quite understandably toughened up its systems on who is allowed in the country. This does not mean that there is less chance of you qualifying for a visa, but it does mean that if you are planning to sidestep your visa conditions you are far more likely to be caught. The consequences can include deportation and not ever being allowed back into the United States.

The general requirements for foreign nationals seeking temporary admission include, but are not limited to, the following:

• The purpose of the visit must be temporary.
• You must agree to depart at the end of your authorised stay or extension.
• You must be in possession of a valid passport.
• You may be required to show proof of financial support.
• You must abide by the terms and conditions of admission.

The US visas that will interest you are either exchange visitor visas, working visas or student visas. All visas in the United States have a letter and number code.

EXCHANGE VISITOR VISAS

The Immigration and Nationality Act (INA) provides two non-immigrant visa categories for people participating in exchange visitor programmes in the US. The J-visa is for educational and cultural exchange programmes designated by the Department of State, Bureau of Consular Affairs, and the Q-visa is for international cultural exchange programmes designated by the Immigration and Naturalisation Service (INS). For example, Rotary exchange students use the Q-visa.

J-EXCHANGE VISITOR PROGRAMME

The J-exchange visitor programme is designed to promote the interchange of persons, knowledge and skills in the fields of education, arts and sciences. Participants include students at all academic levels; trainees obtaining on-the-job training with firms, institutions and agencies; teachers of primary, secondary and specialised schools; professors coming to teach or do research at institutions of higher learning; research scholars; professional trainees in the medical and allied fields; and international visitors coming for the purpose of travelling, observing, consulting, conducting research, training, sharing, or demonstrating specialised knowledge or skills, or participating in organised people-to-people programmes.

There are different categories of the J-visa, with the J1-visa the most commonly applied-for visa for young South Africans wanting a working holiday in the US. The US sees the visa as being part of a cultural exchange with the ability to earn money as a bonus. The visa is for five months, of which four months are for working and one month for travelling in the US. The requirements are not stringent. You must be 18 years old, you must be a student or recently graduated, you may not have a criminal record and you must be able to show that you are genuinely using the opportunity for which the visa is granted.

The US consular sections in South Africa encourage you to work through student organisations. You must, however, check with consular officials that the organisations that you plan to use are recognised by the US authorities. There are some organisations that are not recognised by the United States, which attempt to charge high fees, but do not provide the correct information or assistance.

The recognised organisations will assist you in getting a visa (and advise you if you are wasting your time), with your air flights, assurance, a job and even accommodation. The package includes a few days in New York, where you will be given an orientation course about what you can expect and what is expected from you as a guest in the United States. The choice is yours as to whether or not you organise a job beforehand.

Having a job on arrival is not a requirement. Many people arrange both a job and accommodation when they get there. You need to be careful, as some South Africans, believing they have arranged jobs beforehand, arrive to find that they are either being exploited, or the employer has 'employed' too many people and there is no real job.

Most people taking advantage of the visas work at summer beach resorts or at ski resorts (probably the most popular), or as camp counsellors at summer camps, which are an institution for the youth of America. Many employers supply accommodation, the cost of which is normally deducted from pay. Pay is also often structured to ensure that you remain with the employer for the full contract period, with a bonus being paid at the end of the term. Pay, accommodation and working conditions can vary enormously. For example, at ski resorts, such as Vail in Colorado, some employers may include a season ski pass. Others might include free meals.

WORKING VISAS

These visas tend to be for a longer duration and are designed to fill jobs that US citizens do not want. Most of these jobs tend to be unskilled labour, such as waiters at country clubs. An employer needs to apply for this type of visa on your behalf.

WHERE TO GET MORE INFORMATION

Here are some websites with additional information on US visas: www.state.gov; www.ins.gov; www.ccusa.com.

STUDYING ABROAD

Most countries have special visas for studying abroad. In most cases you will have to study at a recognised institution and be able to pay your fees and living expenses. In the United States, regulations have been tightened as a consequence of the World Trade Center terrorism attack and the flying courses the terrorists took at US flying schools.

Foreign students seeking to study in the US may enter in the F-1 or M-1 visa categories, provided they meet the following criteria:

- The student must be enrolled in an 'academic' educational programme, a language-training programme or a vocational programme.
- The school must be approved by the Immigration and Naturalisation Service (INS).
- The student must be enrolled as a full-time student at the institution.
- The student must be proficient in English or be enrolled in courses leading to English proficiency.
- The student must have sufficient funds available for self-support during the entire proposed course of study.
- The student must maintain a residence abroad, which he or she has no intention of giving up.

Many foreign universities offer bursaries to academically and sports-talented students.

GENERAL ADVICE

The better organised you are, the less likely you are to run into problems. Here are a few tips to help you with your foreign venture:

BEFORE YOU LEAVE

When you start your planning, draw up a checklist of everything you need to do before you leave. This includes:

- Valid passport.
- Visas.
- Return air tickets.
- Travel insurance: You often get travel insurance by using a credit card to buy an air ticket, but you must check the duration and level of insurance. You may need to top up. You can also speak to your travel agent about buying travel insurance, which can last for the duration of your trip. It is particularly useful if you are going skiing.
- Eurail travel card: You have to buy a Eurail travel card or pass in South Africa.
- International student identity card: This card can get you discounts on all sorts of things, from cultural events to entry to museums and art galleries. This can be a major saving.
- International driver's licence: You can get one from the Automobile Association. You need a local driver's licence and do not need to undergo any tests.
- No-claim car insurance: If you intend owning a motor vehicle, get written proof of your no-claim bonus, as this will reduce your car insurance premiums.
- Passport photographs: These are cheaper in South Africa, and you will need them for things such as visa applications and ski passes.
- Pre-book your aircraft seats (try to get the seat you want, whether it is a window seat or an aisle seat. The seat at the emergency exit is a good one). Confirm travel arrangements at least 24 hours before you leave.
- Foreign currency: You should apply for foreign currency a few days in advance. You can take foreign currency in a number of ways, including cash, travellers' cheques and credit card. It is best to use a combination of all three. Larger amounts can also be transferred electronically to a bank in your country of destination.

- References: References, such as from a previous landlord or lady, and a letter of good standing from your bank, will help. A letter from your bank stating that you have been a sound customer will help in opening a bank account. Recent bank statements will also help.
- Documentation: If you have a visa that allows you to apply for a career-oriented job, take CVs and other documentation.
- Hotmail: Arrange a hotmail e-mail address. It will help you to stay in touch while on the move.
- Photocopy all documents, including your passport and travellers' cheques, before leaving. Take one set of photocopies with you and leave another set at home.

WHEN YOU GET THERE

- Try not to behave like a bewildered tourist. Know where you are going. Plan what you are going to do beforehand and have a back-up plan. A bewildered tourist is a good target for a con artist.
- Take care of your possessions, particularly your travel documents and money. You are more vulnerable because you are carrying all your possessions with you.
- Have sufficient money to see you through for at least a month. If you have R20 000 or more, you should be all right. Anything less and you could have problems.
- Your luggage. When travelling, never accept sealed packages from anyone, and keep a close watch on your luggage at all times. In these days of international terrorism and drug cartels you could be placing yourself at tremendous risk by transporting something that may be dangerous. The risks could include penalties, such as a jail sentence and deportation.
- When you get a job, have everything confirmed in writing. Employers, knowing that you are unfamiliar with the systems in the country and that you are there for only a brief period, often promise a lot, but when it comes to the first payday things are not what you thought they were. (Refer to Chapter Seven.)
- Accommodation can be fairly easy to find, but expect to pay more than you would pay in South Africa, both as an actual amount and also as a proportion of your earnings. If you are staying with people as a temporary measure, particularly when you first arrive, be prepared to pay a 'doss' rental. In London, for example, you are expected to pay £5 a night.

- To protect your finances, be prepared to do any work while you are seeking out the job you would like to do. It can sometimes take longer than you expect to find that job, and you will be living off rands in the meantime.

Bibliography

De Kock, Esann. *Personal Finance 60 Minute Guide to Healthcare Finance* (Worth Publishing, 1990).

Cameron, Bruce, and Magnus Heystek. *Retirement – the Amazing and Scary Truth* (Worth Publishing, various editions).

Cameron, Bruce, Alide Dasnois, Charlene Clayton and Esann de Kock. *Personal Finance – The Scrapbook Series* (Worth Publishing, 1990).

Deloitte & Touche. *Pay Less Tax* (various editions).

Divaris, C, and ML Stein. *Old Mutual Income Tax Guide* (various editions).

Downie, James AB. *The Essentials of Retirement Fund Management in South Africa* (Butterworths, annual).

Kourie, MA, and S Keetse. *Tax and Investments Easiguide* (Butterworths, various editions).

SA Department of Finance. *Budget and Budget review documents* (various budgets).

The Life Underwriters Association of South Africa Handbook on Estate Planning (various editions).

Various articles by *Personal Finance* staff. *Personal Finance* newspaper (Independent Newspapers).

Various articles by *Personal Finance* staff. *Personal Finance* magazine (Independent Newspapers).

ZEBRA PRESS
supports

book*eish!*

South African International Festival of Books

Cape Town 27 February to 1 March 2004